YEARS OF

TONY BACON

chronology
compiled by

PAUL DAY

50 years of Fender
Half a Century of the Greatest Electric Guitars

Tony Bacon

A BALAFON BOOK

First British edition 2000

Published in the UK by Balafon Books,
an imprint of Outline Press Ltd,
115J Cleveland Street, London W1P 5PN, England.
www.balafon.dircon.co.uk

ISBN 0-87930-621-1

Printed in Hong Kong

Art Director: Nigel Osborne
Design: Sally Stockwell
Editor: Siobhan Pascoe

Print and origination by Colorprint Offset Ltd,
Hong Kong

00 01 02 03 04 5 4 3 2 1

contents

In 1950 a strange guitar with plank-like body and maple neck emerged from a tin shack in Los Angeles. No one realized its true worth at the time, but this was the birth of a brand new type of musical instrument: the solidbody electric guitar. It would prove revolutionary, providing a new voice for a new music. Leo Fender, owner of the shack, wasn't musical. He'd grown up in Anaheim, in the Los Angeles area. Radios and electronics had become the teenage Leo's passion, and soon he was building small PA systems for local events. At age 30 he opened the Fender Radio Service, a small store in nearby Fullerton where he sold records and sheet music, hired PAs,

and repaired musical instruments. It
was here that he met local musician
Doc Kauffman. Together they built a
testbed guitar to develop pickups,
and formed K&F (Kauffman & Fender)
in late 1945, making electric steel
guitars and small amplifiers. Leo was
happy to work into the middle of the
night in that tin shack at the back of
the radio store, but Doc was less
keen and pulled out a few months
later. So early in '46 Leo set up a new
operation, Fender Manufacturing,
continuing with steels and amps but
gradually developing new products.
This book is about the years and
guitars and schemes that followed,
and the musicians who turned
Fender guitars into great music.

"Fender's first decade was one of brilliant design, the foundation upon which much of the company's subsequent success has been built."

JIMMY BRYANT
prefers a
Fender GUITAR

Broadcasting begins

Fender's electric lap-steel guitars and amplifiers (highlighted in this 1950 catalog, right) enjoyed limited local success, and Leo Fender considered a solidbody electric guitar. This became the Esquire, the Broadcaster, and then the Telecaster. One of the first players to embrace the new Fender was ace West Coast sessionman Jimmy Bryant (above, left), but soon guitarists everywhere would crave Fender electric guitars.

Leo Fender was not entirely alone in his desire to create a solidbody electric guitar. But, crucially, his would be the first commercially available.

Electric guitars had been around since the 1930s, at first mainly steel guitars for playing on the lap, but soon joined by regular hollowbody guitars with crude, early pickups screwed on.

Rickenbacker in California was the first with a pickup employing the electro-magnetic principle since used on virtually every electric guitar, and Gibson set the style for the best hollowbody electrics, offering models such as the fine ES-175 of 1949.

Some musicians and guitar-makers had been wondering about the possibility of a solidbody instrument. It would be without the annoying feedback often produced by amplified hollowbodies, and allow louder playing. It would also be cheaper to produce. Rickenbacker had launched a semi-solid Bakelite-body electric guitar in the mid 1930s. Around 1940 in New Jersey guitarist Les Paul built a test-bed electric with a solid central block of pine. And in 1948 in Downey, California – just 15 miles or so from Leo Fender's base – Paul Bigsby made a solidbody through-neck guitar for country artist Merle Travis.

Leo Fender's new solidbody was the instrument that we know now as the Fender Telecaster, effectively the world's first commercially successful solidbody electric guitar. As we shall see in this book, the design is still very much alive today. The guitar was originally named

the Fender Esquire and then the Fender Broadcaster, and it first went into production in 1950.

It was a simple, effective instrument. It had a basic, single-cutaway, solid slab of ash for a body, with a screwed-on maple neck. Everything was geared to easy production. It had a slanted pickup mounted into a steel bridge-plate carrying three adjustable bridge-saddles, and the body was finished in a yellowish color known as blond. It was unadorned and like nothing else. It was ahead of its time.

Production of the instrument began at Fender's two small steel buildings on Pomona Avenue in Fullerton, Los Angeles, during the first half of 1950. By November, despite serious cash-flow problems, the guitar had a truss-rod and two pickups, and a new name: the Fender Broadcaster.

It did not prove immediately easy to sell. Prototypes taken to a music show were laughed at and disparagingly called canoe paddles or snow shovels. A salesman trying to sell one in San Francisco was offered in exchange the electric train-set of a potential customer's son. It was not an auspicious start for the solidbody electric guitar. However, time would reveal the Fender Broadcaster as one of the most historically significant musical instruments ever made.

This Fender Broadcaster was made in 1950.

Jimmy Wyble of Spade Cooley's band plays a rare early Fender Esquire in this 1950 ad (right).

● *Blond Broadcaster, 1950 retail price: $169.95, equivalent in today's money: $1,200, value of 1950 example now: $17,000*

This 1950 ad (right) was the very first to feature and name the Fender Esquire, Fender's earliest solidbody "electric Spanish" guitar in its pre-production form. It was soon renamed Broadcaster, and finally (in 1951) Telecaster.

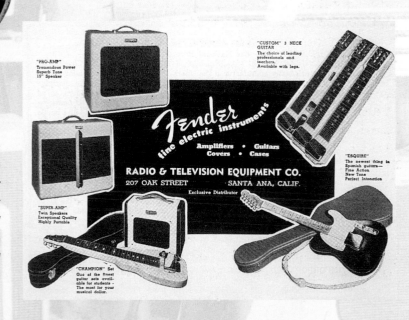

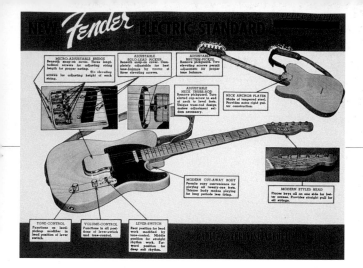

1951

Bass? Precisely.

When Fender introduced a solidbody electric bass guitar at the end of 1951, no one knew what to make of the strange new hybrid. It looked like a long-necked version of the Telecaster, but with four strings, tuned an octave below the lower four strings of a guitar. It was another remarkable innovation from Fender: the world's first commercially-made electric bass guitar. In time it would completely transform the sound of popular music.

Fender started to produce the Fender Precision Bass in October 1951. It shared much of its construction with the Broadcaster, which during 1951 had been renamed the Telecaster. Gretsch, a large New York-based instrument manufacturer, indicated its prior use of "Broadkaster" on various drum products. At first, Fender simply used up its Fender Broadcaster decals on the guitar's headstock by cutting off "Broadcaster," leaving the Fender logo. These instruments are known among collectors today as Nocasters.

The new name decided upon for the two-pickup Fender solidbody was Telecaster (1953 example, far left) while a new single-pickup version re-used the earlier Esquire name (1953 Esquire, near left).

Meanwhile, the new Precision Bass was going into production with a 20-fret maple neck bolted to a pale yellow "blond" ash body. There was a black pickguard and finger-rest, a single-coil pickup, a chromed metal plate under a volume and tone control, and a chromed cover each for the bridge and for the pickup. The bridge had two saddles carrying two strings each, and the strings passed through the body, anchored at the rear.

The Precision was typical of Fender's early products. It had an austere simplicity and was geared to easy, piece-together construction. The tuning of the Fender bass, E-A-D-G, was the same as the double-bass, an octave below the lower four strings of the guitar. This familiarity was designed to attract guitarists looking for a new instrumental skill, as well as double-bass players seeking portability. The electric bass guitar had arrived... though no one took much notice.

The Precision's body design was new for Fender, with an extra cutaway that broke away from the single-cutaway Telecaster and would later inspire the body shape of Fender's Stratocaster guitar. The extra cutaway was needed because the bass's longer neck and heavier tuners would have made a Telecaster-shape design unbalanced. However, by extending the top horn and relocating the strap peg, the balance was effectively restored.

In those years at the start of the 1950s few other guitar companies took seriously Fender's new direction with the electric bass. Forrest White, Fender's production chief from 1954, once said that people who weren't sure if Leo was crazy when he brought out the solidbody guitar were quite certain when they saw the electric bass.

MEANWHILE IN 1951...

DJ ALAN FREED begins an R&B radio program in Ohio. Later Freed claims he invented the term "rock'n'roll" but more likely borrowed it from some of the 45s he played.

ARMISTICE negotiations, which become prolonged, open in Korea during the summer, aimed at halting the war there.

I LOVE LUCY, the definitive 1950s TV sitcom, starts a ten-year run with Lucille Ball as Lucy Ricardo and Desi Arnaz as Ricky the hard-pressed hubby.

LES PAUL & MARY FORD achieve their first number one hit in the US, with 'How High The Moon.'

Jazz bandleader Lionel Hampton (above, left) was an enthusiastic and early endorser of the Precision, persuading his double-bass player Monk Montgomery (below) to adopt the Fender.

• *Blond Precision Bass 1951 retail price: $199.50, equivalent in today's money: $1,310, value of 1951 example now: $5,500*

This Precision Bass was among the first to leave the factory in 1951. The ad (right) was published early in the following year.

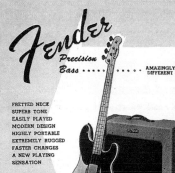

Fender sales head Don Randall (above left) with a Precision at a 1952 show.

1952
Studying the steel

Despite the exciting new developments in solidbody guitars and basses, in the early 1950s Fender's main business was in electric steel guitars and amplifiers. The 1952 ad (above) illustrates this well, showing the early-style "TV" amp cabinets. Later in the year Fender introduced one of its most famous models, the Twin Amp (later catalog, right), which inaugurated a new "wide panel" cabinet style.

Since Leo Fender's days in the mid 1940s running the shortlived K&F company with Doc Kauffman, small instrument-amplifiers and electric steel guitars had been mainstays of his business. These products continued to be vitally important to the new Fender company, and the lines were rapidly expanded.

The steel had been the first type of guitar to go electric in the 1930s, and had become popularized as an easy-to-play instrument suitable for beginners. The electric steel had also gained enormous appeal among professional musicians, especially in Hawaiian music, as well as in country and western bands. The steel guitar was played on the lap or mounted on legs. The name came not from its construction – Fender's steels were all wooden – but from the metal bar used in the player's left hand to stop the raised strings, which were generally tuned to an open chord.

Fender's single-neck steels available before 1950 had included the Organ Button (the odd name derived from its switchable muted "organ"-tone effect), the cheap Princeton with hardwired cord, the long-lived Deluxe which survived in various guises until 1980, and the Champion model. The latter was renamed as the Student in 1952 as a come-on to the booming teaching "studios" of the time. An example of the Student model is pictured opposite.

It was natural for Fender to adapt some of the features of his existing steel guitar designs for the new solidbody instruments. Clearly the Fender Telecaster

and Precision Bass had borrowed stylistic elements from the steel's pickup and cover and the control knobs and plate. In fact, one of the early prototypes for the Esquire/Broadcaster even had the steel's more pointed headstock with three tuners each side, but this was quickly changed to the better known design with six tuners in a line.

Amplifiers too had developed quickly. The pre-1950 Fender line included early wooden-handled Model 26 versions of the Deluxe, Professional and Princeton, as well as an angled-front twin-speaker model, the Dual Professional (soon renamed Super), and a remodeled series in "TV-front" cabinets using the soon famous tweed-pattern cloth covering.

In 1951 along came the Bassman amp, intended to amplify the new Precision Bass but today highly regarded by guitar players. The following year saw another new item, the Twin Amp, this one aimed from the outset at guitarists. It became the top model in Fender's amplifier line, boasting 15 watts output through twin 12" speakers, and all in a new-design "wide panel" cabinet. The grille in this type (see Deluxe, opposite) is squared off and extended further out than the old "TV" style, with wide panels above and below. The whole amplifier line – including Bandmaster, Bassman, Deluxe, Princeton, Pro Amp and Super – was restyled to reflect the new look.

This Student steel model was made in about 1954.

MEANWHILE IN 1952...

FIRST H-BOMB detonation, by the US – many times more powerful than A-bomb – at Eniwetok Atoll in the Pacific.

KING GEORGE VI dies at Sandringham, England, while Princess Elizabeth is away on a Commonwealth tour.

MR. POTATO HEAD becomes the first children's toy to be advertised in a television commercial.

WORLD's FIRST fare-paying jet airliner passenger is Mr. A. Henshaw of Mablethorpe, England, who travels on a BOAC Comet on its first commercial flight from London to Johannesburg along with 35 other passengers.

The Student steel was sold in a budget price set with a matching amplifier (right).

This little Deluxe amp (right) was made with the new "wide panel" cabinet design and covered in "tweed" cloth. The Twin Amp featured in the catalog opposite (top of page) is in the later "narrow panel" style.

Fender
SALES INC.   PRINTED IN U.S.A.

● AMPLIFIERS
● GUITARS
● COVERS
● CASES

308 EAST 5TH ST., SANTA ANA, CALIF.   KImberly 2-8873

1953
Sales & Swing

Fender made multi-neck steel guitars from the earliest days: the two-neck Dual 8 Professional, for example, was launched in 1946, and the triple-neck Custom followed three years later. Multi-neck steel guitars provided players with the means to change quickly between tunings, although the pedal-steel guitar would dispose of this rather unwieldy arrangement. Many of the Western Swing steel players of the 1950s drew their driving electric guitar runs from Fender models such as the Stringmaster.

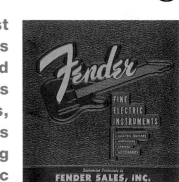

At first, Fender products were distributed by the Radio & Television Equipment Company ("Radio-Tel") which was based in Santa Ana, some 15 miles south of Fullerton. Don Randall was general manager of Radio-Tel, which was owned by Francis Hall.

But early in 1953 the set-up was re-organized into a new Fender Sales distribution company, operational by June. Based like Radio-Tel in Santa Ana, Fender Sales had four business partners: Leo, Don Randall, Francis Hall, and Charlie Hayes.

Hayes, who had been Radio-Tel's first salesman, was killed in a road accident in 1955, while in late 1953 Hall bought the Rickenbacker company. So in 1955 Fender Sales would become a partnership between Leo and Don Randall, though it was Randall who actually ran this pivotal part of the Fender business.

In 1953 Fender had three new buildings put up on a 3.5 acre plot at South Raymond Avenue and Valencia Drive in Fullerton. Clearly expansion of Fender's product lines was imminent.

As well as just two electric guitars, the Telecaster and Esquire, Fender had at this time a line of seven amplifiers (Bandmaster, Bassman, Champ, Deluxe, Princeton, Super, Twin Amp), five electric steel guitars in various versions (Custom, Deluxe, Dual, Stringmaster, Student) and its revolutionary electric bass guitar, the Precision.

But clearly the company wanted to make more models. *The Music Trades* magazine reported in 1953

that with the new property Fender hoped that production would be upped by almost 100 per cent in the next few months. A significant new project begun in 1953 would turn into Fender's best known instrument, the Stratocaster. An important addition to the Fender team occurred in 1953 with steel guitarist Freddie Tavares, principally to help Leo design new products. Freddie and Leo worked together developing plans for the new solidbody Strat. But for the time being it was Western Swing that was bringing the electric guitar to popularity in the US. Western Swing was a lively dance music that had grown up in Texas dancehalls during the 1930s and 1940s.

Many of Western Swing's steel-guitar players used Fender electrics, notably Noel Boggs with Spade Cooley and Leon McAuliffe with Bob Wills. But there were also some "Spanish" guitarists in the ranks, such as Telecaster-wielding Bill Carson with Hank Thompson's Brazos Valley Boys. However, Fender's days of reliance on its steel guitar lines was soon to end. Business began to pick up for the company as news of the solidbody "Spanish" Telecaster and Esquire spread among guitarists, and as the new Fender Sales got into gear and its salesmen – soon growing to Art Bates, Mike Cole, Dave Driver, Charlie Hayes, and Don Patton – began to persuade more instrument-store owners to stock Fenders.

TAKE IT AWAY *Leon*

MEANWHILE IN 1953...

CLOCK RADIOS are introduced, bringing news like the end of the Korean war and Queen Elizabeth II's coronation.

CRAZY MAN CRAZY by Bill Haley & His Comets, number 12 in the US, is arguably the first hit rock'n'roll record.

COLOR TV is demonstrated for the first time.

LUNG CANCER is linked to cigarette smoking – but L&M still plug their cigarettes as "just what the doctor ordered."

MICROWAVE OVEN patented by Raytheon company of US.

JAMES BOND debuts in Ian Fleming's novel *Casino Royale*.

DEAD: Django Reinhardt, Dylan Thomas, Joseph Stalin.

Fender's Stringmaster steel of 1953 (below) had two, three or four eight-string necks. This example may have been owned by Leon McAuliffe (above), the great steel player who'd joined Bob Wills's Texas Playboys at age 18.

FENDER

Bill Carson (right) is seen playing a Telecaster in Hank Thompson's outfit, which played a commercial fusion of Western Swing and honky tonk. The band had a big hit with 'The Wild Side Of Life' in 1952. The line-up pictured here dates from 1953.

HANK THOMPSON and his BRAZOS VALLEY BOYS
Nation's No. 1 Western Recording Artist Recording exclusively on Capitol Records

Nation's No. 1 Western Swing Band.

Strataclysmic

Leo Fender listened hard to players' comments about the Telecaster and Esquire models, and during the early 1950s he and Freddie Tavares began to devise the guitar that would become the Stratocaster (seen in stylized form on the 1954 catalog cover, right). At first other makers had merely mocked Fender's new solidbody guitars, but soon Gibson had joined in with its Les Paul, Gretsch with the Duo Jet, Kay with its K-125. Competition was looming – and Fender needed to up the stakes. This they most certainly did.

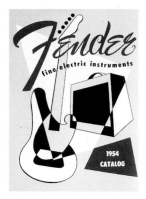

The Stratocaster was launched during 1954. Samples around May and June were followed by the first proper production run in October. The new Fender guitar was the first solidbody electric with three pickups, meaning a range of fresh tones, and featured a new-design vibrato unit that provided pitch-bending and shimmering chordal effects.

The new vibrato – erroneously called a "tremolo" by Fender and many others since – was troublesome in development. But the result was the first self-contained vibrato unit: an adjustable bridge, a tailpiece, and a vibrato system, all in one. It wasn't a simple mechanism for the time, but a reasonably effective one. It followed the Fender principle of taking an existing product (in this case, the Bigsby vibrato) and improving it. Fender's new vibrato had six bridge-pieces, one for each string, adjustable for height and length, which meant that the feel of the strings could be personalized and the guitar made more in tune with itself. The complete unit was typical of Fender's constant consideration of musicians' requirements and his application of a mass-producer's solution.

The Strat came with a radically sleek, solid body, based on the outline of the 1951 Fender Precision Bass. Some musicians had complained to Fender that the sharp edge on the Telecaster's body was uncomfortable – the dissenters included musician/entertainer Rex Gallion and Western Swing guitarist Bill Carson – and so the Strat's body was contoured for the player's comfort. Also, it was finished in a yellow-to-black sunburst finish.

Even the jack socket mounting was new, recessed in a stylish plate on the body face. And the headstock? Side by side with Paul Bigsby's guitar made for Merle Travis in 1948 there is clearly influence from the earlier instrument. But as a whole the Fender Stratocaster looked like no other guitar around, especially the flowing, sensual curves of that beautifully proportioned, timeless body.

The Stratocaster's new-style pickguard complemented the lines perfectly, and the overall impression was of a guitar where all the components ideally suited one another. The Fender Stratocaster has since become the most popular, the most copied, the most desired, and very probably the most played solid electric guitar ever. On its 40th anniversary in 1994 an official estimate put Strat sales at over a million guitars. At its launch it wasn't such a world-beater; later in the 1950s the Strat began to hint at future glories, especially in the hands of players like Buddy Guy, Carl Perkins, and Buddy Holly.

Eldon Shamblin (right) was an early Strat player, with Bob Wills's Texas Playboys.

This non-standard-color 1954 Strat is serial 0001.

MEANWHILE IN 1954...

THE US has 6% of the world's population, but 34% of its railways, 58% of the telephones, and 60% of the cars. TRANSISTOR RADIOS are introduced, made by Regency. DOO-WOP heaven as The Spaniels make 'Goodnight Sweetheart Goodnight' and The Penguins record 'Earth Angel.' Meanwhile, Elvis Presley makes his first recordings. IN THE UK, post-war food rationing officially ends, celebrated by a bonfire of ration books in London. In the United States the term "fast food" comes into use. WEST GERMANY wins the soccer World Cup.

Early Strat instruction book.

● Sunburst Stratocaster, 1954 retail price: $249.50, equivalent in today's money: $1,590, value of 1954 example now: $18,000

Cool cat (above) with Strat and new "narrow panel" Twin Amp. Standard finish for the Strat was sunburst, like this '56 example (right). Bill Carson poses with an early Fender Stratocaster (left). Carson contributed ideas to the Fender team working on the new guitar.

BILLY CARSON *uses* **Fender** Fine Electric Instruments Exclusively

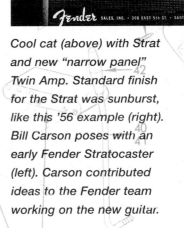

speaking for cats everywhere

Fender SALES, INC. • 308 EAST 5th ST. • SANTA ANA, C

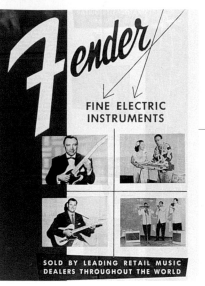

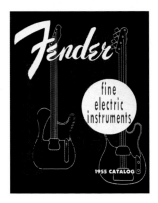

Switched-on Tremolo

Fender's new Strat did not have an immediate impact, and only later in rock'n'roll did it find its true home. For the time being, Fender continued to advertise its established lines – including the Telecaster and Precision Bass, pictured on the covers of the two 1955 catalogs shown here (above and right). Steel guitars continued virtually unchanged, but innovations were still being made with Fender's ever-popular amplifiers.

Forrest White was a new and important addition to the Fender ranks at this time. He was in effect the head of production, and gradually organized the somewhat haphazard working methods into a more efficient and effective operation. White had already met Leo a few times when, in spring 1954, the two had lunch and

Leo asked Forrest if he'd be interested in helping to sort out a number of what he described as "management problems" at Fender. Leo knew that the operation was close to collapse. Sometimes Fender checks would bounce locally: Leo had no credit and often had to pay cash for materials. White's timing was perfect, and he joined the company.

Forrest White helped to turn things around, along with Don Randall who was busy bolstering sales, and Freddie Tavares who was Leo's main ideas man in the design of new amplifiers and guitars.

Guitarist Bill Carson was still among the musicians whose views were sought by the Fullerton-based Fender team when designing the new products that any manufacturer must continually produce. Carson would often take out prototype amplifiers for testing and evaluating at local gigs, leaving the unit with other players for a while so that he could monitor a range of opinions to feed back to the factory. Leo would sometimes appear at the gigs, walk right up to the amp, mid-song, and – oblivious to the musicians –

begin to fiddle with settings. Carson has said that none of the musicians particularly relished Leo's visits, and considered him "a pest."

One of the new amplifier effects being developed was what Fender called "tremolo," a regular, rhythmic fluctuation in volume, previously heard on home organs. The model that introduced the effect to the Fender amplifier line was the Tremolux, a 15-watt amp with single 12" speaker. It was launched in 1955. One of the tubes in the Tremolux's circuit was used as an oscillator in order to provide the distinctive tremolo sound, which could be switched on and off as required by the player. But this reallocation of tube duty did limit the power output of the amp. As the circuitry improved, tremolo would become a popular amplifier effect, not least in the work of players such as Link Wray and Duane Eddy.

Fender's amplifiers in 1955 ranged from the top-of-the-line 50-watt Twin Amp, now in classic "narrow panel" style and with two 12" speakers, priced at $279.50, down to the 4-watt Champ (sometimes called Student) with 6" speaker at just $59.50.

At the bottom of the steel guitar pricelist sat the humble Student (the renamed Champion model), but this was replaced in 1955 by the Champ, a more straightforward design with straight body sides, retaining the single slanted Telecaster-style pickup and simple volume-and-tone controls.

The Champ steel was also sold as a set (right) with an amp for around $120.

MEANWHILE IN 1955...

ROSA PARKS, a black bus-passenger in Montgomery, Alabama, defies a segregated seating rule when she refuses to give up her seat to a white person.

JAMES DEAN is killed in a car crash.

DISNEYLAND is opened in Anaheim, Los Angeles. Walt Disney originally planned to call it Mickey Mouse World.

CHUCK BERRY and Bo Diddley cut their debut records, on the Chess and Checker labels.

NON-STICK cooking pans introduced by Tefal in France.

McDONALD'S second store opens, in Des Plaines, Ohio.

This Champ steel guitar was made around 1958.

Steel guitarist Pete Drake went on to play with Bob Dylan, including the sessions for Nashville Skyline.

The Tremolux amplifier was the first Fender to feature the new "tremolo" effect, a rhythmic volume fluctuation.

Schoolroom guitars

Just as rock'n'roll began to rise in the US, Fender shifted its electric guitar line downwards. The company launched two new low-end electrics, the Duo-Sonic and the Musicmaster, specifically to cater for the army of beginners enlisted by music stores keen for a new customer base. A solidbody electric Mandolin (left) was also new in the company's catalog (above), while ads (right) continued to stress Fender's existing lines.

A common marketing method to increase sales of guitars and many other musical instruments during the 1950s was the "school" or "studio," usually run at musical instrument stores after-hours and offering lessons to would-be players. Naturally such a school was well situated to sell a start-up instrument to the beginner... and equally attentive when the new musician felt his or her skills demanded a better and more expensive instrument with which to show off this new-found talent.

Fender was as aware of these marketing tactics as any go-ahead American instrument manufacturer and

sales outfit of the time. So it was that the company introduced in 1956 a pair of new "student" electrics. These two new instruments – the Duo-Sonic and the Musicmaster — had a shorter 22½" (571mm) scale-length as opposed to Fender's customary 25" (635mm) scale. The "three-quarter size" one-pickup Musicmaster and two-pickup Duo-Sonic were described in the company's ads and catalogs as being "ideal for students and adults with small hands."

They were clearly designed for players on a tight budget, for those starting out on electric guitar who flocked to the retailers' schools. The two new guitars certainly looked cheaper than Fender's Stratocaster,

Telecaster, and Esquire – and indeed they sat at the bottom of Fender's pricelist. Around this time the Strat with vibrato listed at $274.50, the Tele at $199.50, Esquire at $164.50, Duo-Sonic at $149.50, and the Musicmaster at $119.50.

One apparently attractive feature of the Duo-Sonic and Musicmaster (and a few early Stratocasters) was what Fender called "gold-finished pickguards." These 'guards were in fact made from a gold-colored anodized aluminum. The metal provided excellent electrical shielding, meaning less extraneous noise. However, the electrolytic anodized "skin" soon wore through to the aluminum below as the player strummed and picked, leaving unsightly gray patches. The anodized 'guards did not last much beyond the 1950s.

Rock'n'roll burst on to the scene in 1956, and players like Carl Perkins at Sun and Paul Burlison in The Rock'n'Roll Trio (sleeve, left) seized on the bright, cutting sound of Fender's solidbody electrics. But Fender looked back to a traditional instrument for its other new model for 1956: the electric Fender Mandolin. It sold for $169.50, with a Fender-style double-cutaway solid body and four strings rather than the regular mandolin's eight (in four pairs). Perhaps surprisingly, the Mandolin lasted in the line until the mid 1970s.

Fender described the Duo-Sonic and Musicmaster (right) as three-quarter size. The neck (and scale-length) was shorter than other Fenders.

New Fender *Musicmaster* Three-quarter Size Electric Standard

Fender
fine electric instruments

Distributed Exclusively by
FENDER SALES INC.

Most Fenders came with point-of-sale material such as this instruction booklet.

Fender
Duo-Sonic
AND
Musicmaster
INSTRUCTION MANUAL

This blond Duo-Sonic with anodized pickguard was made in 1959.

You won't part with yours either*

Where musicians go, you'll find Fender!

Fender
SALES INC.
1536 EAST CHESTNUT

FEBRUARY, 1959

Fender's classic "You won't part with yours either..." ads began in the 1950s. The new Musicmaster (1957 example, far right) features in this school scene (right).

G2I-1-A

3

Low-note heaven

It was becoming clear that rock'n'roll was not only going to change popular music for good, but that it would also have a fundamental effect upon the fortunes of the Fender company. Buddy Holly's 1957 debut album *The Chirping Crickets* (above) visibly declared to a growing band of fans his preference for the Fender Stratocaster. And in studios and stages across America the newly configured Fender Precision bass was beginning to provide a new, solid foundation for a brand new music.

Some makers had joined in after Fender had marketed the first electric bass guitar in 1951 – Kay in 1952, Gibson in 1953, Danelectro in 1956 – but popular use of the electric bass guitar still remained scarce. The emerging rock'n'roll music at first stayed in the hands of double-bass players: Al Rex with Bill Haley's Comets, Joe B. Maudlin with Buddy Holly's Crickets, and Bill Black with Elvis Presley. However, Black got a Fender Precision around 1957: he certainly had one in the MGM studios during the filming of *Jailhouse Rock*, and Presley's title track recorded in April sounds as if it features Black on Fender. This stamp of approval was important for Fender's basses, and many fellow players noted Black's adoption of the new-fangled electric bass guitar.

By 1957 Fender basses were being seen more frequently on stage. Contemporary photos reveal a Precision in the live bands of Jerry Lee Lewis and B.B. King, among others. Looking back now, it seems remarkable that the electric bass took so long to become established. Fender had made some minor changes to the design of the Precision in 1954, contouring the body and painting it in two-tone sunburst like the Strat. But in 1957 some more fundamental changes were made. Most important was a brand new split-coil pickup with a more defined and solid bass sound. Fender also redesigned the shape and bulk of the instrument's headstock, enlarging it to help overall balance as well as to improve resonance and the uniformity of individual notes.

It was unusual for Fender to make such major changes to an existing production model, and indicated that the company was still searching for a combination of features that would appeal to and attract the new breed of electric bassists. A more minor change was the new-shape Precision pickguard, which at first was of the anodized aluminum type. These final alterations of 1957 – new pickup, larger headstock, different pickguard – defined the look of the Precision for decades to come.

Fender also announced early in 1957 a Strat in see-through blond finish and gold-plated hardware. This was later called the "Mary Kaye" thanks to musician Kaye appearing with one in a number of Fender catalogs of the period (example, far left, alongside a blond/gold Strat). The gold-hardware blond-finish Strat was Fender's first official Custom Color guitar – although the term has been more popularly applied since to solid-color varieties. As we shall see, Fender eventually came up with a defined list of Custom Colors.

Fender Sales bought a Piper aircraft in 1957 so that Don Randall (above) could pilot cross-country sales trips.

MEANWHILE IN 1957...

SOVIET UNION launches Sputnik II in orbit around the earth with a dog on board, proving that life can survive in space.

JACK KEROUAC launches the Beat Generation with his novel *On The Road*.

WOLFENDEN REPORT in the UK calls for homosexual acts between consenting adults to be decriminalized.

ON THE BEACH by Nevil Shute is published, a horrific vision of worldwide nuclear devastation.

TV DEBUTS include *Wagon Train* and *Perry Mason* in the US, and *Emergency Ward 10* and *Six-Five Special* in UK.

Fender began making pedal-steel guitars in 1957. The catalog (below) shows the 400 and 1000 models; Speedy West (sleeve below) was a fine 1000 user.

This Precision Bass was made during 1957.

Donald "Duck" Dunn (left) was a keen Precision player. Dunn gained fame in the 1960s with Booker T & The MGs.

The new Fender Electric Violin has proved advantageous to every musician playing amplified violin for solo, group and orchestra work. It is the result of numerous experiments by Fender engineers to amplify with fidelity true violin tone . . . neither adding to or taking from the sonority of this remarkable instrument.
It employs fine violin craftsmanship including the expertly positioned ebony fingerboard and neck designed to the specifications of the finest instruments. It is extremely lightweight and comfortable to play with the tone and volume controls and input jack positioned so that none interfere. The tone control provides for effects heretofore unattainable in achieving natural tonal blends with other instruments. Volume may be varied from the softest to greatest volume response without limitation. Only the tone and volume settings of the amplifier used limit the response of the Fender Electric Violin.
The instrument is beautifully made of choice grained woods, finished in Sunburst and fitted with chinrest, fine-tune patent heads and bridge. Leading violinists who have played the new Fender Electric Violin acclaim the advancement in amplified violin qualities represented by this instrument. It is an instrument with beauty of tone, beauty of design and one which will satisfy the most discriminating violinist. It opens an entirely new field and is the answer to every violinist's desire for an instrument possessing the refinements and tone characteristics of violin amplification.

Fender ELECTRIC VIOLIN

Jazzy circuitry

With Musicmaster and Duo-Sonic established at the bottom of the pricelist, Fender now tried to expand the high-end, introducing the new Jazzmaster during 1958. Never the most popular Fender, the Jazzmaster did at least offer the first glimpse of a Fender rosewood fingerboard, soon adopted for other models. Altogether more unusual was the Fender Electric Violin that also debuted in 1958.

For its next model introduction Fender created a distinctly high-end instrument. The Jazzmaster first appeared in Fender sales material during 1958, and at some $50 more than the Strat it became the new top-of-the-line model. Fender could not resist tagging the new Jazzmaster as "America's finest electric guitar... unequalled in performance and design features."

Immediately striking to the electric guitarist of 1958 was the Jazzmaster's unusual offset-waist body shape, which became the subject of one of Fender's now growing number of patents. For the first time on a Fender, the Jazzmaster featured a separate rosewood fingerboard glued to the customary maple neck, aimed to give a more conventional appearance. The Jazzmaster's floating vibrato system was new, too, and had a tricky "lock-off" facility aimed at preventing tuning problems if a string should break.

The controls were certainly elaborate for the time, and at first were set in one of Fender's "gold" anodized pickguards. A small slide-switch selected between two individual circuits, offering player-preset rhythm and lead sounds. The idea was a good one: the ability to set up a rhythm sound and a lead sound, and switch between them. But the system seemed over-complicated to players brought up on straightforward volume and tone controls.

The sound of the Jazzmaster was richer and warmer than players were used to from Fender. The name Jazzmaster had not been chosen at random, for

Fender was aiming this different tone at jazz players, who at the time largely preferred hollowbody electrics, and principally those by Gibson.

However, jazz guitarists found little appeal in this new, rather difficult solidbody guitar – and mainstream Fender players largely stayed with their Stratocasters and Telecasters.

The Jazzmaster certainly marked a change for Fender, and constituted a real effort to extend the scope and appeal of the company's guitar line. Ironically, and despite some early successes, this has been partly responsible for the Jazzmaster's lack of long-term popularity relative to the Strat and Tele, mainly as a result of players' dissatisfaction with the guitar's sounds and playability. A limited resurgence of interest came with punk in the 1970s and, later, grunge.

After the electric solidbody Mandolin, Fender could not resist trying its electric approach with another traditional instrument – the violin. The Fender Electric Violin debuted in 1958, with a solid maple body, special pickup, and typical Fender-style controls and jack. The Fender-shape headstock was routed with a single slot to reveal the tuner spindles. Despite high hopes for this "advancement in amplified violin qualities" Fender withdrew the Violin after less than a year. However, it did reappear in slightly modified form in the late 1960s for a rather longer run.

Roy Lanham (right) played a Jazzmaster on his instrumental LP. In the early 1960s Lanham joined Leo Fender's favorite group, the Western singing outfit Sons Of The Pioneers.

This Jazzmaster was made in 1959. Here (right) are some original tags.

● *Sunburst Jazzmaster, 1958 retail price: $329.50, equivalent in today's money: $1,950, value of 1958 example now: $3,500*

The Jazzmaster figured strongly in Fender's continuing "You won't part with yours either..." ad series.

Reacting to criticism that its guitars were plain, Fender introduced the new bound-edge sunburst Custom Telecaster and Custom Esquire. Custom Color Fenders were also appearing more often, and the 1958/59 catalog was Fender's first with a color cover (above), a Fiesta Red Strat prominently displayed. The company was still keen to experiment, resulting in one-offs such as this see-through amplifier (right) made for a trade show.

During all the changes and additions to the Fender line in its first decade, the humble Telecaster – in effect Fender's first solidbody electric guitar – had stayed almost exactly the same. Cosmetic alterations included a change from the original black to a white pickguard at the end of 1954 (like the example in the 1959 ad, left). But otherwise the Telecaster was largely the same blond-finished guitar it had been in 1951. Some 1950s Telecasters had been made in non-standard colors, and a few small batches had been finished in sunburst. In 1959, however, two new models joined the Fender line that gave a quite different look when compared to the continuing regular Telecaster and the single-pickup Esquire. These were the Custom Telecaster and the Custom Esquire. Each had a sunburst-finish body with bound edges. Binding is a technique that creates a thin white strip on the edge between the top and sides and back and sides of the guitar, and was more often seen on hollowbody guitars such as those made by Gibson.

The new Customs also had rosewood fingerboards, as on the Jazzmaster. During 1959 the new separate rosewood fingerboard on a maple neck was adopted for all the other existing Fender models – regular Telecaster and Esquire, Stratocaster, Duo-Sonic, and Musicmaster. It replaced Fender's previous construction that laid frets directly into the face of a solid maple neck.

Guitarists in Britain had been unable officially to buy any US-made guitars since 1951 when a ban on imports had been imposed. However, enterprising singer Cliff Richard had approached the Fender factory in California in 1959 after his guitarist, Hank Marvin, had pointed out the strange concoction known as a Fender Stratocaster pictured on a Buddy Holly record sleeve. Marvin was soon the owner of the first Stratocaster in the UK, and his group The Shadows displayed it to thousands of adoring fans as Cliff and the group began their rise to fame. During 1959 the import ban was lifted, and US guitars could once again be legally sold in Britain.

A new amplifier, the Vibrasonic, introduced some fresh features to the Fender line in 1959. It had a new style of cabinet with a sloping, front-mounted control panel, and was finished in a hard-wearing vinyl material, Tolex, that replaced Fender's classic "tweed" linen covering.

The regular Telecaster and Esquire models (right) continued in the Fender line.

MEANWHILE IN 1959...

BUDDY HOLLY is killed in a plane crash in Iowa along with fellow passengers Richie Valens and The Big Bopper. RUSSIA launches Lunik I into planetary orbit around the sun, lands Lunik II on the moon, and uses Lunik III to take the first photographs of the dark side of the moon. BMC's £500 Mini, "the people's car" designed by Alec Issigonis, is launched in the UK. The Volvo PV544 is the first car equipped with a three-point adjustable seat belt. IN CUBA, dictator Fulgencio Batista is overthrown by a revolutionary movement under Fidel Castro.

This Custom Telecaster was made in 1963.

The first Strat in the UK: pictured here; with Cliff Richard (right) and Jayne Mansfield in 1959; and with Shadows man Hank Marvin (below).

Fender's flyer (far left) illustrates the Custom Tele (standing) and the Custom Esquire. The American family at home on the 1959/60 catalog cover (left) has mom clutching the headstock of a Custom Telecaster.

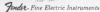

"As rock music exploded with electric guitars at the core, Fender provided perfectly malleable tools for the new sonic revolutionaries."

Now color me Jazz

Fender's fine new electric bass guitar was the Jazz Bass model. It brought a new level of luxury to the Fender bassist and produced a wider tone, largely a result of its new pair of eight-pole "strip" pickups. Bright news for Fender's Custom Color fans was a newly prepared chart that illustrated samples of all the available color options (above), while over in Britain the new Fender distributor published its first advertisement (right).

The new Fender Jazz Bass began to appear from the factory in March 1960. Having established with the ground-breaking Precision that the bass guitar was an important new instrument with a unique voice that would help to define pop music, the next step for Fender was to make an upscale model.

The design of the Jazz Bass was distinguished by its offset-waist body, similar in style to the Jazzmaster guitar launched two years earlier. The Jazz Bass also differed from the Precision in its narrow string spacing at the nut, which gave the neck a distinctly tapered feel, and its provision of two pickups which offered wider tonal possibilities. For many years the Precision Bass would outsell the more expensive Jazz Bass: some

preferred the out-and-out simplicity of the Precision; others opted for the crisper tones and different feel of the Jazz. The pickups of the Jazz Bass were connected in humbucking mode, as was the "split" pickup used on the Precision since 1957. Leo Fender later explained to several interviewers that in the 1950s Fender never emphasized the humbucking capabilities of these pickups because the company's patent attorney had told them that such pickups had been patented back in the 1930s. Leo explained that

humbuckers were introduced on the basses because he thought the earlier single-coil pickup was too hard on the amp's loudspeakers, whereas the humbucking types offered a softer, less spiky signal – no doubt easing the Fender amp-repair department's workload.

Pop groups began to emerge in the early 1960s with all-guitar line-ups (plus drums), a significant change that would benefit Fender enormously. In the US one of the leading instrumental bands was The Ventures. While they later moved to a business relationship with Mosrite guitars, for the first few years they played Fenders, as gloriously displayed on early sleeves (far left). In the UK the top instro group was The Shadows. They are seen with singer Cliff Richard in the first UK ad for Fender guitars (top), placed in 1960 by Fender's new British distributor Jennings (who also marketed Vox amps).

Fender's Custom Colors reached an important new level in 1960 when the company's first color chart (top left, alongside a 1960 Fiesta Red Telecaster) was issued. Fender used paints by Du Pont – a big supplier to America's car factories – including the Duco nitro-cellulose lines, such as Fiesta Red or Foam Green, as well as the more color-retentive Lucite acrylics, like Lake Placid Blue Metallic or Burgundy Mist Metallic.

At first the Jazz Bass had two "stacked" control knobs, as on this early flyer (right). Later versions had three controls.

This Teal Green Jazz Bass dates from 1964. Fender sold Regal-brand guitars (below) around 1960.

● *Sunburst Jazz Bass, 1960 retail price: $279.50, equivalent in today's money: $1,610, value of 1960 example now: $8,000*

Two artful Fender catalogs (right) with early Jazz Basses.

Bob Dylan plays

Fender
MUSICAL INSTRUMENTS

Bobby seen (left) in the basement, mixing up the Jazz Bass. An unlikely sight, maybe, but Fender put out this intriguing ad around 1967.

Between a regular guitar and a bass dwelt the six-string bass, introduced as the Fender VI model in 1961. This year also saw the rise of surf music, personified by Dick Dale (the left-hander with the Strat, top). Years later Dale's distinctive Strat (on the sleeve, above) would prompt a signature model from the modern Fender operation. Back in 1961, Fender amplifiers split into "piggyback" form with the new Showman.

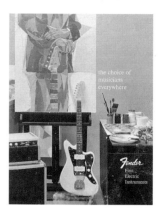

The New Jersey-based Danelectro company had produced the first six-string electric bass guitar in 1956. Guitarists were the target for this new instrument – effectively an electric guitar tuned an octave lower – and the different sound of the Dan'o appealed to players like Duane Eddy as well as to some studio musicians. Other makers noted the popularity, and Fender launched its take on the idea with the VI in 1961. The scheme was to offer an instrument to guitarists who wanted a bass sound: the VI was a guitar with a longer neck, its strings tuned an octave lower than a regular guitar.

Fender's VI (often referred to as the Bass VI) was a specialist instrument, and as such never proved especially popular. Probably its best-known user was British bassist Jack Bruce who briefly used one in his early Cream days later in the 1960s. Some VIs still turn up today in studios for a particular sound, but the tight string-spacing makes them of limited appeal to bass players.

Fender still understood the value of visual appeal to grab attention at the trade shows it now regularly attended, and after the see-through amplifier of the previous year built a Duo-Sonic with a transparent plastic body (left) for exhibition at the annual NAMM (National Association of Music Merchants) show. A number of other similar see-through Fenders were produced around this time.

Guitar-based pop groups were multiplying at a rate that must have satisfied Fender Sales, with instrumental outfits becoming particularly popular. Dick Dale headed one faction when he became known as the "king of the surf guitar." Left-hander Dale (Dick and band, plus his distinctive Strat, are pictured at the top of the page) poured out surging, staccato lines, borrowing scales from an East European heritage, all set adrift in a sea of reverb. His big hit was 1961's 'Let's Go Trippin,' but surf music didn't last much beyond the British invasion of 1964.

In the amplifier department at Fender a new kind of set-up was introduced with the "piggyback" Showman rig. This had the electronics housed in a separate box that sat on top of the separate speaker cabinet: a familiar arrangement now, but new at the time. Also new to the 1961 Fender line was reverberation ("reverb") created with a vibrating spring. The effect had been developed by the Hammond organ company for home instruments. At Fender, it first appeared in the separate Fender Reverb unit, but a few years later made its way into amps such as the Vibroverb as a switchable effect.

This later 1960s catalog (right) details various VI features, including the guitar's newer four-switch control panel.

MEANWHILE IN 1961...

THE TWIST is the latest dance craze. Less rhythmically bound, Bob Dylan debuts in New York folk clubs and is signed to the Columbia record company.

CATCH-22 is Joseph Heller's comic-surreal novel about American airmen in the wartime Mediterranean.

YURI GAGARIN is the first man in space. A month later Alan Shepherd is the first American catapulted up there.

THE BERLIN WALL is built to prevent East Berliners reaching the West. Elsewhere the contraceptive pill goes on general sale, aimed to control more personal incursions.

This VI was made in 1962 – still with the original three-switch panel.

A number of amps, including the Showman, changed to Fender's new "piggyback" two-piece style in 1961.

A later 1960s catalog page (left) reveals a VI (second from right) with features such as a four-switch panel and block-shape fingerboard markers.

A spin in the Jag

Not content with the relatively expensive Jazzmaster, Fender introduced a new top-of-the-line model in 1962: the Jaguar. Another offset-waist multi-control instrument, the Jag seemed an attractive proposition, but still failed to dent the supremacy of Fender's dynamic duo, the Tele and the Strat. Steve Cropper (above) of Booker T & The MGs showed just how effective the noble Tele could be in the right surroundings.

The next new guitar to leave Fender's production line was the Jaguar, which first showed up in sales material during 1962. The Jag used a similar offset-waist body shape to the earlier Jazzmaster, and also shared that guitar's separate bridge and vibrato unit, although the Jaguar had the addition of a spring-loaded string mute at the bridge. Fender rather optimistically believed that players would prefer a mechanical string mute to the natural edge-of-the-hand method. They did not. There were some notable differences between the

Jaguar and Jazzmaster. Visually, the Jag had distinctive chromed control panels, and was the first Fender with 22 frets. Its 24" (610mm) scale-length ("faster, more comfortable") was shorter than the Fender standard of 25" (635mm) and closer to that of Gibson. It gave the Jag a different playing feel compared to other Fenders. The Jaguar had better pickups than the Jazzmaster. They looked much like Strat units but had metal shielding added at the base and sides, no doubt as a response to the criticisms of the Jazzmaster's tendency to noisiness. The Jag's electrics were yet more complex than the Jazzmaster's, using the same rhythm circuit but adding a trio of lead-circuit switches.

Like the Jazzmaster, the Jaguar enjoyed a burst of popularity when introduced. But this new top-of-the-line guitar, "one of the finest solid body electric guitars that has ever been offered to the public" in Fender's original sales hype, never enjoyed sustained success, and has always been marked down as an also-ran.

The Jaguar was offered from the start in four different neck widths, one a size narrower and two wider than normal (coded A, B, C or D, from narrowest to widest, with "normal" B the most common). These neck options were also offered from 1962 on the Jazzmaster and Strat.

In the studio, cool-hand Steve Cropper (pictured at top left of this page) translated the good old Telecaster's simplicity of design into musical terms as his lean guitar lines graced 1962's Booker T & the MGs hit, 'Green Onions.'

From around 1960 in its print advertising Fender had begun to use a modernized "chunky" Fender logo that had been drawn up by Bob Perine, the man responsible for the stylish look of Fender's advertising from the late 1950s to the late 1960s. The Jaguar was the first standard electric guitar to carry the new logo on its headstock. During the following years Fender gradually applied it to all models. In this incarnation (early to mid 1960s) it has become known among collectors as the "transition" logo because it leads from the original thin "spaghetti" Fender logo to a bolder black version introduced at the end of the 1960s.

the most imitated guitar in the world

Another amusing "You won't part with yours either" ad (right), this one illustrating the crucial gigging-by-motorcycle test.

MEANWHILE IN 1962...

TELSTAR, a communications satellite, is launched, enabling the first live TV transmissions between Europe and the US.

NELSON MANDELA is jailed in South Africa and gets a life sentence in 1964 that results in his internment until 1990.

CUBAN MISSSILE CRISIS starts as Russia sites rockets in Cuba. An American blockade of Cuba is only lifted when the Soviet Union removes the missiles.

ANDY WARHOL is among the pop artists in the New Realists exhibition in America. "In the future," says Warhol, "everyone will be famous for 15 minutes."

This Jaguar in Candy Apple Red was made in 1964. The Jag ads here came out during the 1960s.

● *Sunburst Jaguar, 1962 retail price: $379.50, equivalent in today's money: $2,160, value of 1962 example now: $1,800*

Carl Wilson of The Beach Boys (left) was one of the most prominent players of the Jaguar in the 1960s. Fender's no-expense-spared matchbox promotion (inset) must also have boosted the Jag's fortunes, though the model has never matched the Strat and Tele for that classic Fender playability and style. Which may explain why Al Jardine clutches a Strat.

Fenders with air inside

Fender became so excited about the prospect of making its own acoustic guitars that it poached a guitar-maker from fellow California company Rickenbacker, and created a new factory in which to build them. Unfortunately, that enthusiasm did not translate into guitars to match Fender's great solidbody electrics. This year also saw the introduction of the first Fender-Rhodes electric pianos.

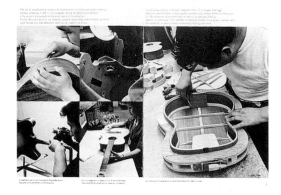

Like most guitar operations in the United States in the 1960s, Fender wanted to expand its market share. It was simply not considered enough to be at the forefront of solidbody electric guitar production. But some players felt that the company had taken a step too far when its first acoustic flat-top guitars were announced during 1963.

Fender had marketed flat-top acoustics before. In 1959 the Harmony company of Chicago first supplied Regal-brand equipment for exclusive distribution by Fender, including flat-top acoustics and the R-270 archtop electric. Evidently this arrangement did not prove successful, and the Regal lines were dropped in the early 1960s. Roger Rossmeisl was brought into the company by Leo Fender to design the company's own new flat-top acoustic guitars and to oversee their construction. The acoustics were manufactured at a new plant on Missile Way in Fullerton, about a mile from the main Fender factory.

Rossmeisl was the son of a respected German guitar-maker, Wenzel Rossmeisl, and had come to the United States in the 1950s. At first he had worked for Gibson in Michigan, but soon moved west to Rickenbacker in California. There Rossmeisl's skills became more evident, and he made a number of one-off custom guitars as well as designing production models for Rickenbacker's distinctive Capri and Combo series.

Rossmeisl's work also influenced other makers, notably Mosrite of California.

For the Fender acoustics, Rossmeisl gave the instruments the outward look of conventional flat-tops, but for most of them he retained the heel-less bolt-on neck that had served Fender so well for its solidbody electrics. Thus the necks had an "electric" feel, as opposed to the wider necks of most flat-tops.

Rossmeisl also began to fit many of the Fender acoustics with an aluminum support rod inside the body, designed for maximum rigidity. A patent for this "acoustic tension tube" was granted in 1968. Fenders with the tension-tube feature, visible through the guitar's soundhole, are sometimes called "broomstick" models.

The first steel-string acoustic models were the King (later renamed Kingman) and Concert, launched in 1964. There were also steel-string Folk and nylon-string Classic models that had conventional acoustic-guitar construction. The King had Martin's much-emulated "dreadnought" wide-shouldered body shape. Later introductions to the flat-top series included the Shenandoah and Villager 12-strings, as well as the Malibu, Newporter, Palamino, and Redondo models. None of these would prove especially popular, but some of these first acoustics stayed in the Fender line until the early 1970s.

A collection of Fender acoustics prepare to frolic in the California surf (right).

MEANWHILE IN 1963...

PRESIDENT KENNEDY is assassinated in Dallas, Texas. MARTIN LUTHER KING speaks in Washington. "I have a dream," he says, "that my four little children will one day live in a nation where they will not be judged by the color of their skin but by the content of their character." UK POLITICIAN John Profumo resigns after his involvement with Christine Keeler, mistress of a Soviet naval attaché. "SEXUAL INTERCOURSE began in 1963, (Which was rather late for me) –, Between the end of the Chatterly ban, And the Beatles first LP." That's how poet Philip Larkin saw it.

This Palomino in Mahogany finish was made around 1970.

Rick Nelson (top, left) and Johnny Cash (above) pose with Fender acoustics.

The 1963/64 catalog cover features the new "blackface" Twin Reverb amp (right).

Mustang savvy

As Fender tinkered with its low-end models and Custom Colors, musical revolutions were taking place. The Beatles had begun their moves to world domination, branching out spectacularly from local British stardom. And the trend in the UK for young white groups to play black R&B saw 'Little Red Rooster' by Howlin' Wolf (sleeve, right) provide a perfect blueprint for The Rolling Stones.

A new model was added this year by Fender at the lower end of its pricelist. The Mustang was in effect the $159.50 Duo-Sonic with a vibrato added – for which Fender added an extra $30 over the price of the Duo-Sonic. The Mustang shared the generally low-end features of the earlier Duo-Sonic, as well as its two single-coil pickups.

At first, the Mustang also shared the "slab" body of the Duo-Sonic – unrefined, squared-off edges without much thought of the player's comfort. But over the next few years Fender gradually introduced a contoured body to all of its "student" models: one-pickup Musicmaster, two-pickup Duo-Sonic, and vibrato-equipped Mustang.

While the existing Duo-Sonic and Musicmaster had previously been available only with a short scale of 22½" (571mm), from 1964 these models too were made available in optional medium-scale 24" (610mm) versions. The medium-scale models were known as the Musicmaster II and the Duo-Sonic II. Other minor changes were made to the two existing budget models to make them more stylistically similar to the new Mustang. The Mustang was also offered in two different scale-lengths, though short-scale Mustangs were rarely ordered and few were built.

The optional Custom Colors scheme for many models was now well underway, and a new color chart had been issued in 1963. Available colors were Black, Burgundy Mist Metallic, Candy Apple Red Metallic,

Dakota Red, Daphne Blue, Fiesta Red, Foam Green, Inca Silver Metallic, Lake Placid Blue Metallic, Olympic White, Sherwood Green Metallic, Shoreline Gold Metallic, Sonic Blue, and Surf Green. Fender used paints from Du Pont's Duco nitro-cellulose and Lucite acrylic lines which had been developed primarily for use by automobile manufacturers. The names that Fender gave to its Custom Colors came from the original car makers' terms. Fiesta Red, for example, was first used by Ford in 1956 for a Thunderbird color, while Lake Placid Blue originally appeared on a 1958 Cadillac Brougham. When Gibson had copied Fender's idea of Custom Colors for its Firebird series, one of the finishes – a coppery gold – was identical to a Fender shade. Gibson adopted its Oldsmobile name, Golden Mist, because Fender already used the Pontiac term, Shoreline Gold.

Decades later the guitars bearing these original Fiesta Reds, Sonic Blues, and Burgundy Mists, especially from the late 1950s and the 1960s, have proved very collectable. A Custom Color Fender, especially an early one, is rated a prime catch. And this despite the prevalence of recent "refinishes," so good they can fool many an alleged expert.

Happiness in Hawaii (right) with a Mustang or two for this carefree catalog scene.

Fender 1965

This Mustang was made around 1972.

- 'spaghetti' logo Strat, in Burgundy Mist, 1964 retail: $303.97 (today's money: $1,670), value of 1964 example now: $13,000
- Lake Placid Blue Precision Bass, 1964 retail: $240.97 (today's money: $1,330) value of 1964 example now: $4,500
- Foam Green Jazzmaster, 1964 retail: $366.97 (today's money: $2,020) value of 1964 example now: $4,000

CUSTOM FINISHES FOR *Fender* FINE ELECTRIC INSTRUMENTS

Three desirable Custom Color guitars (above): a 1961 Strat in Burgundy Mist; a Lake Placid Blue Precision Bass; and a Jazzmaster in Foam Green (the last two both made in 1963).

The catalog (left) shows how the Duo-Sonic (center) had been slightly altered this year to match the new Mustang (far left).

Fender
SALES, INC.

Suddenly it's CBS

Fender was sold to CBS at the very start of this year, and for many of the company's fans things would never be the same again. At first the prospects seemed good as the new owner pumped money and enthusiasm into the impressive purchase. But in years to come the relationship would be soured. None of this stopped Fender introducing new models, although the new instruments released for 1965 – the Bass V and the Electric XII – proved shortlived.

Since the launch of the humble Broadcaster in 1950, Fender had turned into an extremely successful company. The rock'n'roll revolution saw the company churning out good, relatively affordable guitars available in large numbers. Fender had captured a significant portion of the new market. Many buildings had been added to cope with increased manufacturing demands, and by 1964 the operation employed some 600 people (500 in manufacturing) spread over 29 buildings. As well as electric guitars, Fender's pricelists offered amplifiers, steel guitars, electric basses, acoustic guitars, electric pianos, effects units, and a host of related accessories.

Sales boss Don Randall remembers writing a million dollars' worth of sales during his first year in the 1950s, which rose to some 10million dollars' worth in the mid 1960s (translating to some $40million of retail sales). Electric guitars were at their peak of popularity, and Fender was among the biggest and most successful producers, selling its products in the US and well beyond. Players as diverse as surf king Dick Dale, bluesman Muddy Waters and pop stylist Hank Marvin – plus thousands of others around and between them – were rarely seen without a Fender in their hands. However, Leo Fender was by all accounts a hypochondriac, and his acute health worries (as well as

uncertainties about financing expansion) prompted him to sell Fender. Don Randall handled the sale.

In January 1965, Fender was sold to the mighty Columbia Broadcasting System Inc – better known as CBS. The purchase price was a staggering $13million, by far the highest ever paid in the musical instrument industry for a single manufacturer. In fact, it was about $2million more than CBS had recently paid for the New York Yankees baseball team. CBS executive Goddard Lieberson said of Fender: "This is a fast growing business tied into the expanding leisure time market. We expect this industry to grow by 23 per cent in the next two years." CBS went on to buy other instrument companies such as Rogers (drums), Steinway (pianos) and Leslie (organ loudspeakers).

While the shock of the change set in – and the sale was to have far-reaching consequences – the Electric XII and Bass V (far left) were launched. The V was an unusual, shortlived 15-fret five-string bass, with a high C-string. Electric 12-strings had recently been popularized by The Beatles and Byrds, both with Rickenbackers. Fender's version was belated. An innovation was the 12-saddle bridge for precise adjustments of individual string heights and intonation. But the 12-string craze of the 1960s was almost over and the Electric XII also proved shortlived, lasting in the line only until 1969.

This Electric XII in Candy Apple Red was made in 1966.

MEANWHILE IN 1965...

RUSSIAN cosmonaut Alexei Leonov is the first man to "walk" in space, leaving his Voskhod II craft for 10 minutes.

AMERICAN TROOPS go on their first offensive against the Vietcong. By July there are 125,000 US troops in Vietnam.

CARNABY STREET is the center of Swinging London, selling op-art mini dresses, PVC boots, and colored tights.

THE SOUND OF MUSIC achieves irritatingly widespread popularity. One reviewer warns moviegoers who are "allergic to singing nuns and sweetly innocent children."

A SPEED LIMIT of 70mph is imposed on UK motorways.

Electric XIIs book-end a trio of Teles at this 1969 catalog session (below).

The 1965/66 catalog (right) showed early prototypes of the ill-fated Marauder with "Invisible" pickups (under the pickguard). Further protos like the one pictured here had multiple switches and angled frets, but neither type made it into production.

Another surrealistic wallow (left) for the Fender ad team.

F is for f-holes

The Coronado guitars and basses, intended as competition for arch-rivals Gibson, were launched by Fender in 1966. They proved once again that Fender ought to stick with solidbody instruments, and none was successful. A cheaper bass model, the Mustang Bass (left), was also added to the line. Pop music was becoming ever more adventurous, and players like Jeff Beck (right) in The Yardbirds and Robbie Robertson with the newly-electric Bob Dylan were confirmed Fender fans.

The Coronado thinline guitars were yet more creations from Roger Rossmeisl's Missile Way acoustic factory, and the first electric hollowbody designs to appear from Fender. Clearly, the company was being pushed by new owners CBS to compete with the successful 300-series thinline electrics marketed by the other big name in the guitar market, Gibson.

The Coronados looked like conventional competitors for the Gibson models, with equal-double-cutaway bound bodies that sported large, stylized f-holes. But in fact, just like the earlier flat-tops, they employed the standard Fender bolt-on necks, as well as the company's distinctive headstock design. Options

included a new vibrato tailpiece, and there was a 12-string version that used the Electric XII's large curved headstock design. Unfamiliar with some edge-binding techniques, factory hands had to re-do some of the work. To cover up burn marks caused by re-binding, the team devised a special white-to-brown shaded finish – Antigua – to salvage the scorched Coronados. Antigua-finish Coronados would go on sale over the next few years.

In 1967 Fender introduced even more unusual colored versions of the Coronados, the Wildwoods. As pop culture became absorbed with the dazzling, drug-influenced art of psychedelia, Fender predictably announced the Coronado Wildwoods as "truly a happening in sight and sound" with "exciting rainbow hues of greens, blues and golds."

They certainly did look different. The Wildwood effect was achieved by injecting dyes into beech trees during growth, producing in the cut wood a unique colored pattern which followed the grain. Despite all the fuss, the feedback-prone Coronados never caught on, and the various versions would be dropped from the catalog by 1971.

Fender's first short-scale four-string, the Mustang Bass, did little to expand or enhance Fender's line beyond the company's leading bass duo. The type shown (top left) is the later Competition version, distinguished by contrasting colored stripes on the body.

Over in England, Jeff Beck had struck an early blow for the coming pre-CBS cult – the deification of guitars made before the CBS takeover in 1965 – when he bought a 1954 Esquire and began using it with The Yardbirds. The picture (top right of this page) shows the Esquire before he switched the white pickguard for a "correct" black one and moved a notch higher in one-upmanship among vintage-conscious guitarists on the scene. Beck played it on 1966's 'Shape Of Things' 45 among a jukeboxful of others.

Spanish is the acoustic tongue in this 60s ad (right).

MEANWHILE IN 1966...

SAN FRANCISCO is the hippie capital of the world. The Psychedelic Shop opens on Haight Street, and the Avalon Ballroom is the grooviest rock venue.

LONDON is the fashion capital of the world: Biba on Kensington Church Street, John Stephens on Carnaby Street, Mary Quant on Kings Road are the "in" stores.

THE PHILIPS "Musicassette" is established as the industry-standard medium for cassette recording.

LENNY BRUCE, comedian who assaulted unmentionable subjects (sex, race, religion, politics...), is dead at 40.

This Wildwood Coronado II was made in 1968. Coronados (below) in Wildwood (far left and right) and Antigua (second left) shown in a late-1960s catalog, plus Wildwood color samples.

WILDWOOD COLORS *(Color and grain varies slightly with each instrument.)*

Wildwood I
Rainbow Greens

Wildwood II
Rainbow Blues

Wildwood III
Rainbow Golds

Chris Hillman (far left) and Roger McGuinn of The Byrds pop by for their Wildwood Coronados, but secretly plan to use only the amps.

1967
Solid state? Illogical.

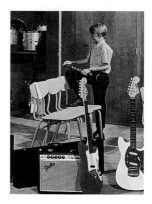

Catastrophe hit Fender this year as the first Solid State amps went on sale – and then many quickly came back as unworkable. It was one of the first signs that CBS might not be acting in the best interests of the many musicians who relied on Fender products. In England, George Harrison harmonized psychedelia and rockabilly with his custom-painted "Rocky" Strat (left).

Fender launched another of its "student" solidbody electrics this year, the $149.50 Bronco with single pickup and simple vibrato, along with a matching amp. The new guitar was the cheapest in the line, other than the Musicmaster, and lasted in the catalog until the early 1980s. In this lowly area of its pricelist Fender seemed reasonably assured, though elsewhere, as we've seen, uncertainty was creeping in. But amplifiers had always been a safe and reliable part of the company's business. There was of course much more competition now compared to Fender's earliest days, but players generally liked Fender amps – and even if they didn't choose the brand, they admired and respected it.

However, with the new Solid State line, first sold in 1967, Fender made its first big amplification mistake. Internal arguments developed over the project, and in the turmoil Forrest White – who had joined Leo in 1954 – resigned.

Solid state electronics, driven by transistors rather than the conventional tubes, were new and, it seemed at the time, the way to go. Various other makers were introducing solid state amps, and Fender decided it had to join in, despite the squabbling.

Problems were legion as the first models – Solid State Deluxe Reverb, Solid State Pro Reverb, Solid State Super Reverb, and Solid State Vibrolux Reverb – came off the line in 1967. The factory struggled with unfamiliar electronics work, and the repair department was piled with returns. The ultra-clean sound of the amps that did work was at odds with the kind of distortion-laden music that players such as Jimi Hendrix were popularizing at the time. To many, this part of Fender's line seemed dangerously out of touch. The Solid State amps were dropped by 1970. Fender's strengths were, thankfully, more than enough to rise above such a disaster.

One of the few top bands apparently absent from Fender usage was The Beatles, who in their concert days had contented themselves with an on-stage mix of primarily Epiphone, Gibson, Gretsch, Hofner, and Rickenbacker guitars. Now that they were strictly a studio outfit, other brands had crept into the arsenal, including Fender. George Harrison and John Lennon each acquired a Strat in 1965 for studio use – heard to stinging effect on cuts of the period such as 'Nowhere Man' – and Paul McCartney bought an Esquire around 1967 for six-string recordings. Also this year, Harrison painted his existing Strat with a wild "Rocky" decoration (see top of page), in time for appearances in the band's *Magical Mystery Tour* TV movie. It could hardly go unnoticed.

The new Bronco guitar and amplifier (right) ignored by kids fighting for the steels.

MEANWHILE IN 1967...

ROLLING STONE magazine is launched in San Francisco. "THE 14-HOUR Technicolor Dream" is staged at London's Alexandra Palace, and 10,000 attend the all-night happening that includes Pink Floyd and a fiberglass igloo. ISRAEL defeats an Arab coalition in the Six Day War. THE BBC bans The Beatles' *Sgt Pepper* track 'A Day In The Life' because of alleged "drug references." THE MONTEREY POP FESTIVAL boasts a line-up that includes The Who, The Byrds, Jefferson Airplane, Janis Joplin, Jimi Hendrix, and Otis Redding.

Since the 1950s Muddy Waters had used a Telecaster (seen on this 1967 album, below) for his electric blues.

This Bronco in standard Red finish was made around 1972.

Various examples of Fender's disastrous Solid State amplifiers are pictured in late-1960s catalogs (below), while workers at the factory (left) take time out from Ronettes tribute bands to assemble the new electronic circuits.

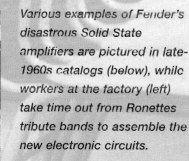

1968
PsychoTelec...

As psychedelia arrived in the shape of the Blue Flower and Pink Paisley Telecasters, original bluesmen like Buddy Guy (right) were helping to inspire a continuing craze in the US and Europe for blues-rock. Fender's product catalogs continued to develop under the control of adman Bob Perine, seen at the camera (left) during the photoshoot for the company's impressive 1968 brochure (above).

The Telecaster had become a dependable instrument for players in many different kinds of music, but in country the Tele had become almost a membership badge. It was admired and put into regular service in the country capitals in Nashville and on the West Coast, offering a simplicity that encouraged the voice and character of the individual guitar player to shine out.

During the late 1960s Fender tried a number of variations on the Telecaster. For example, in 1968 psychedelia hit Fender when self-adhesive wallpaper with a paisley or floral pattern was applied to some Telecasters, presumably in order to give them fresh flower-power appeal.

Certainly the Paisley Red and Blue Flower Teles and Tele Basses could not be described as examples of CBS's boring approach to guitar design. But the Tele seemed the least likely target for the creation of such far-out psychedelic art objects. Since its inception in the early 1950s, the model had rarely been seen without its standard blond finish, even though Custom Colors were offered. However, the dazzling wallpaper experiment did not last long. While the company did not immediately seem to grasp the fact, it would nonetheless gradually dawn on Fender that a central part of the Telecaster's lasting appeal is its strong resistance to change.

Another unusual pair of guitars made a first appearance in 1968. Roger Rossmeisl had been let loose with a couple of guitar designs that were even less like the normal run of Fenders than the earlier Coronado models. Rossmeisl's specialty was the so-called "German carve" taught to him by his father, Wenzel. It gives a distinctive indented "lip" around the top edge of the body, following its outline. Rossmeisl adopted this feature for the new hollowbody archtop electric Montego and LTD models (LTD left; Montego opposite). Both were eminently traditional, yet again obstinately using Fender's customary bolt-on neck.

From all reports there were very few Montegos and LTDs made, and it has been suggested that some of those which did manage to reach music stores may subsequently have been recalled to the factory because of constructional problems. Rossmeisl had an alcohol-related problem at this time, and did not last much longer working for Fender. He died back home in Germany in 1979 at the age of 52.

Some amplifiers began to display a small cosmetic change this year, adopting a new aluminum control panel. These are now known among collectors as "silverface" models to distinguish the color of their control panels from the "blackface" style that preceded them.

This Paisley Red Telecaster was made around 1968.

MEANWHILE IN 1968...

MARTIN LUTHER KING is shot dead in Memphis, and Senator Robert Kennedy is assassinated in Los Angeles.

FRENCH STUDENTS riot and a general strike is called in support, but Communists lose in landslide Gaullist victory.

2001: A SPACE ODYSSEY has Sixties movie audiences enthralled by a tale from ape-man to space station.

SOVIET and Warsaw Pact forces invade increasingly liberal Czechoslovakia, re-imposing totalitarianism.

VIETCONG's sustained "Tet Offensive" attacks on Saigon make victory by South Vietnamese and US seem less likely.

Roger Rossmeisl designed several new electric hollowbody guitars launched in 1968, including the Montego II (right) and the LTD (opposite page).

The steely Tele of Clarence White (right) featured on The Byrds' country-flavored album Sweetheart Of The Rodeo.

FENDER'S *Blue Flower*

Blue Flower bursts forth in a dazzling array of subtle purple and green patterns. Never before has such an exciting profusion of color been offered. *Telecaster $279.50, Telecaster Bass $289.50.*
(These finishes are available on the Telecaster and Telecaster Bass only.)

Fender
MUSICAL INSTRUMENTS

There were two options for the psycho Telecaster and Telecaster Bass: Paisley Red, or Blue Flower (left).

1969
Custom clunker

The Woodstock festival marked the end of the 60s. Half a million music lovers were cast in a sea of mud, entertained by musical luminaries such as Jimi Hendrix (above), ablaze with musical passion and communicating through his white Fender Stratocaster. "Musicians want to pull away after a while," he said, "or they get lost in the whirlpool." A year later he was dead at 27.

Two "new" guitars provided firm evidence of CBS wringing every last drop of potential income from unused factory stock that would otherwise have been written off. The shortlived Custom (also known as Maverick) and Swinger (or Musiclander) were assembled from modified leftovers.

The Custom used discontinued Electric XII necks and bodies, converted to six-string use and with slightly reshaped body and headstock. The Swinger was made from unused Musicmaster or Bass V bodies that were mated with unpopular short-scale Mustang necks, again with the body reworked, and with the headstock turned into a spear-like point.

Both were made in necessarily limited numbers. The Swinger never featured in Fender's sales material, but was a low-end model at any price. The Custom was a little more evident, listing at $299.50 – a few dollars more than a regular Telecaster of the period.

Leo Fender's services had been retained by CBS as "special consultant in research and development." CBS didn't want Leo taking his ideas elsewhere, but equally didn't want him getting in the way of the newly efficient Fender business machine. So he was set up away from the main operation and allowed to tinker as much as he liked – with very little effect on the Fender product lines.

A couple of years after the sale to CBS, Leo recovered from his illness that had provoked the sale of Fender in the first place. He completed a few

projects for CBS, but would leave when his five-year contract expired in 1970. He went on to make instruments for the Music Man company (originally set up in 1972, though not named Music Man until 1974) and his G&L operation (founded in 1979). Leo Fender died in 1991.

But Leo had not been the first of the old guard to leave CBS. As we've seen, Forrest White departed in 1967 in the midst of arguments over the solid state amps. White died in 1994. Don Randall resigned from CBS in 1969, disenchanted with corporate life, and formed Randall Electric Instruments, which he sold in 1987. George Fullerton left CBS in 1970, worked at Ernie Ball for a while, and with Leo formed the G&L company in 1979, although Fullerton sold his interest in 1986. (G&L at first stood for "George & Leo.")

As the close of the 1960s loomed, Stratocasters took a boost when an inspired guitarist by the name of Jimi Hendrix applied the guitar's sensuous curves and glorious tone to his live cavorting and studio experiments. Fender salesman Dale Hyatt: "When guys like that came along, we couldn't build enough guitars. As a matter of fact, I think Jimi Hendrix caused more Stratocasters to be sold than all the Fender salesmen put together."

Fender introduce a fresh meaning for the word "new" in this Custom ad (right).

MEANWHILE IN 1969...

CONCORDE makes its first flights in France and Britain, but the supersonic airliner does not fly commerically until 1976.

NEIL ARMSTRONG is the first man to step on to the moon.

BRITISH TROOPS begin patrolling Catholic areas of Belfast as unrest and violence erupt in Northern Ireland.

BRIAN JONES, founder of The Rolling Stones, drowns at home in his swimming pool.

IN VIETNAM comes the first major withdrawal of US troops.

PAUL BLEY, jazz pianist, is the first professional musician to perform to a live audience playing a synthesizer.

This Custom (main guitar) was made in 1970. A sort of six-string XII with a Mustang vibrato, it was also made as the Maverick (headstock, left). Fender's 1969 ad (above, right) shows the Custom alongside striped Competition Mustangs and a Tele with an f-hole, the new Thinline.

The Swinger (1969 example, here) was another CBS "bitser" made from leftover parts. The headstock shape would turn up 16 years later on Fender's Performer.

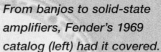

From banjos to solid-state amplifiers, Fender's 1969 catalog (left) had it covered.

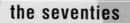

"Fender survived the Seventies by shunning innovation, concentrating instead on the production of its core models in vast quantities."

No frets, please

As Fender entered the 1970s there was little sign of successful innovation. Instead, management seemed increasingly content to settle on old designs and allow those to provide the major income. It was a time of musical change, too, as the heady experimentation of the 1960s subsided and pop music itself divided into yet more factions. Many would later look back on the 1970s as the least satisfying decade in Fender's history, yet as we shall see there was still much to intrigue and fascinate.

In 1966, the New York-based Ampeg company had launched the first fretless bass guitar. The instrument's smooth, unfretted fingerboard enabled bassists to achieve a sound completely different to that of the fretted instrument. Notes "swell" with a beautifully

warm tone, and the fretless player can more easily execute slides. Among the earliest well-known players of fretless bass guitar was Rick Danko of American folk-rock pioneers The Band. Danko primarily played fretted Fenders, but was given some instruments by Ampeg around 1970, including a fretless bass which he quickly modified with Fender pickups. Perhaps it was this that finally spurred Fender to offer a fretless version of the Precision Bass from 1970, at the same price ($293.50) as the regular fretted model. The company also added a new bass to the bottom of its pricelist in 1970, the Musicmaster Bass, another short-scale instrument, pitched at $139.50.

The Beatles' last ever "concert" was played on the rooftop of the band's Apple HQ in London, and featured in the 1970 movie *Let It Be* that effectively charted their break-up. George Harrison played a Rosewood Telecaster, an unusual and shortlived all-roscwood model that had been launched by Fender the previous year. The exotic Rosewood Tele was made

from a timber more usually regarded as suitable only for guitar fingerboards. It makes for a striking yet heavy instrument – and Fender attempted to lighten the load of later versions by moving to a two-piece construction with hollowed chambers inside. It is said that two special Rosewood Stratocasters were also made at this time: one was a prototype; the other was apparently intended for Jimi Hendrix, but the presentation was never made.

Fender's Don Randall had been successful in securing a meeting with The Beatles at Apple some time before the famed rooftop concert. This resulted in the band receiving various Fender products: some Fender-Rhodes pianos, a Jazz Bass, and a VI six-string bass, as well as the Rosewood Tele – all of which are visible at various times during *Let It Be*.

While Eric Clapton had started out with Fenders in The Yardbirds, he soon changed allegiance to Gibsons, which he used to great effect through the 1960s with John Mayall and with Cream. But when in 1970 he recorded the impressive *Layla* album, the change of pace was reflected in a new choice of guitar: a Fender Stratocaster, as pictured on the back of the record's sleeve (see top of page). This began a lengthy and productive relationship between Clapton and Strat, leading to a popular Fender signature model in the 1980s.

This Fretless Precision Bass was made about 1973.

MEANWHILE IN 1970...

APOLLO 13 lands safely after a complex rescue operation followed near-fatal pressure losses and fuel cell failure.

AMERICAN forces bomb North Vietnam after two-year halt.

RHODESIA severs its last tie with Britain and declares itself a racially segregated republic.

FOUR STUDENTS are shot dead at Kent State University as National Guardsmen open fire during a demonstration that questions America's new involvement in Cambodia.

DIVORCE becomes legal in Italy.

THE BEATLES split; Jimi Hendrix and Janis Joplin are dead.

George Harrison (right) played a Rosewood Telecaster (1969 example, right) in The Beatles' famous rooftop appearance in the 1970 movie Let It Be.

Fender's Musicmaster Bass was also sold as a set with a matching amp, as seen on this 1970 catalog page.

Thinlines and neck-tilts

Fender was not yet finished with the idea of a guitar that strayed into Gibson territory. However, the Thinline Telecaster ended up pleasing neither Fender nor Gibson aficionados, and did not survive the 1970s. Alterations were aimed at the Strat, which gained a three-bolt neck fixing and "bullet" truss-rod adjuster, while the number of players attracted to this and Fender's other classics was increasing all the time.

It had become obvious to the management at CBS/Fender that the experiments with hollowbody guitars – the flat-tops, electric thinline Coronados, and full-body Montego and LTD – had not been successful. Most had by now been quietly dropped from the line.

However, the company had pressed forward with another plan to gain some of the market from rivals such as Gibson who were dominating hollowbody electrics. This time, Fender took one of its finest existing models, the Telecaster, and produced a Thinline version, beginning in 1968. Roger Rossmeisl's Thinline Telecaster design had three hollowed-out cavities inside the body and a modified

pickguard shaped to accommodate the single, token f-hole. At first the instrument retained the regular Telecaster pickup layout – one single-coil at the neck, plus another in the distinctive slanted position on the bridge plate. But in 1971 the Thinline Telecaster was given a new pickup layout, with two new Fender humbuckers. Humbucking pickups had two coils wired in such a way that the noise often associated with single-coil pickups was cancelled. At this time most players would have thought that Fender meant single-coil pickups while Gibson meant humbucking pickups. The new humbucker-equipped f-hole

Thinline Telecaster was clearly designed to send a signal that Fender was invading Gibson territory. But it only underlined that players still wanted identifiably Fender guitars from Fender.

It was also around this time – and quite apart from Fender – that Byrds guitarist Clarence White and drummer Gene Parsons had come up with their "shoulder strap control" B-string-pull device that fitted into a Telecaster, designed to give string-bends within chords to emulate pedal-steel type sounds. Elsewhere, Fender's musical stock was high: from Eddie Hazel's slicing Strat in Funkadelic (sleeve, above) to Jimmy Page's anthemic Telecaster break on Led Zeppelin's 'Stairway To Heaven' (*Zep 4* sleeve, left) and the low-key but refined Strat work of Steve Winwood (Traffic sleeve, top left).

Starting in 1971, two primary changes were made to the Strat. The adjustment point for the truss-rod was moved from the body-end of the neck to the headstock, with a new "bullet"-shaped adjuster. A neck-tilt mechanism was also added, adjustable at the neck-plate, and the neck/body joining screws (nearly always called bolts) were reduced from four to three. These were reasonable changes in themselves, but other problems due to increased production and some sloppy quality control has colored the reputation of these 1970s Strats.

This Thinline Telecaster was made in 1972.

MEANWHILE IN 1971...

FIRST SPACE STATION, Salyut, launched by Soviet Union.

BRITAIN'S MONEY changes from the old £-s-d units (pounds-shillings-pence) to a new decimal system.

GENE VINCENT, Louis Armstrong, and Duane Allman die.

A COURT rules that George Harrison's 'My Sweet Lord' has "unconsciously plagiarized" The Chiffons' 'He's So Fine.'

INTERNMENT without trial is introduced in Northern Ireland as violence continues. An explosion at the Post Office Tower in London wrecks three of its floors.

THE FILLMORE EAST and Fillmore West rock venues close.

The "bullet" truss-rod adjuster at the headstock (right) was also made a feature of the Strat from 1971.

The original Thinline Tele of 1968 (example, right) had regular Tele pickups, as in this ad (above).

Back in 1971 most people were unaware that Fender's first solidbody had debuted in 1950: hence the ad (right).

● *Sunburst Stratocaster, three bolt fixing, 1971 retail price: $367.00, equivalent in today's money: $1,550, value of 1971 example now: $1,900*

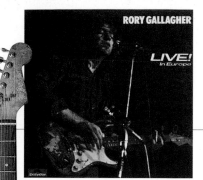

Return to bass

Humbuckers were dished out to a number of models in the line, including the existing Telecaster Bass. This had been the first Fender reissue, designed to recreate the look of the original Precision Bass. Now, however, the Tele Bass was saddled with one of the new humbuckers. A new Martin-like look was adopted for the Japanese-made F series flat-tops (catalog cover, right) that had debuted at the end of the 1960s.

Taking a look back to the original styling of the Precision Bass, Fender had come up with the Telecaster Bass in 1968. This was a significant occurrence, not so much for the instrument itself, but because it was the first time that Fender had effectively "reissued" an earlier design. Many more would follow.

The Telecaster Bass aped the maple neck, slim headstock, pickguard shape (if not color), control panel, and indeed virtually the entire general visual style of the original pre-1957 Precision Bass.

Quite why Fender came up with this reissue, however, remains something of a mystery. The Precision Bass was continuing to sell in very healthy numbers, and the new Telecaster Bass was actually pitched a few dollars higher. Standard-finish basses at the time listed for $356.50 (Jazz Bass), $302.50 (Telecaster), $293.50 (Precision), $239.50 (Mustang), and $139.50 (Musicmaster). To clutter a price-point with two models in this way was unlike Fender. Perhaps it was simply an example of an instrument that seemed like a good idea at the time?

Whatever the motivation, Fender changed the look of the Telecaster Bass in 1972 by adding one of the new humbucking pickups, a pair of which had been added to the Thinline Tele last year. The new-look Tele Bass now had little in common with the original-look Precision, and the idea of reissuing classic Fender designs went back on the shelf for some time. Fender reconsidered the effect of its wholesale replacement of single-coil pickups with humbuckers on the Thinline Tele, and came up with a different arrangement for the Telecaster Custom in 1972.

This time the classic Tele lead pickup, mounted in the bridge-plate, stayed put, and just the neck pickup was changed to a humbucker – a relatively common modification at the time for some players who wanted a wider range of sounds from their Telecasters.

Like many Fenders of the period, the Telecaster Custom was fitted with a bullet truss-rod adjuster and the neck-tilt system. It also came with the company's new high-gloss "thick skin" finish, achieved by spraying more than a dozen coats of polyester on to the unfortunate instrument, and today much despised by some for its plastic appearance and giveaway 1970s vibe. Some models in the line were also offered in Natural ash as a Custom Color from 1972.

Blues-rock was still alive and well, and one of its finest exponents and an international blues hero was Ireland's Rory Gallagher. His battered 1961 Strat (pictured, top of page) was his trademark guitar, the original sunburst body down to bare wood almost everywhere, with a much-refretted fingerboard that responded perfectly to Gallagher's nimble fingers. The guitarist continued to promote the blues with an intense passion until his untimely death in 1995.

Another Strat lover was Richard Thompson, who'd left Fairport Convention and made his first solo LP (right).

This Telecaster Bass was made in 1972.

The original Telecaster Bass (1968 example, right) was Fender's first "reissue," launched as a re-creation of the early Precision.

The F Series flat-top acoustics had first appeared in the late 1960s, but this year were changed in style.

Numbers or quality?

As guitars poured out of Fullerton, great music continued to be fueled by Fenders. Spoilt for choice, we'll pluck just two of the great albums from this year. The Isley Brothers made *3+3* (left), featuring Ernie Isley's flowing, Hendrix-flavored Strat weaving its way among the songs, while *Countdown To Ecstasy* by Steely Dan (below) had guitarists Denny Dias and Jeff Baxter dueling brilliantly on Strats and Teles and more.

Part of Fender's distinction had come from using bright-sounding single-coil pickups. The warmer, fatter-sounding humbucking types were always seen then as a mainstay of Fender's principal rival, Gibson. Nonetheless, as we've seen over the last few years, Fender tried to keep abreast of changing market trends, and various models had been fitted with humbuckers. Fender had in fact hired a key Gibson engineer to devise its new humbucking pickups. Seth Lover had been enticed to California in 1967, away from the Gibson company in Michigan where Lover

had famously invented Gibson's humbucking pickup in the 1950s. Warm, powerful humbuckers had given a distinctive edge to dozens of Gibson models, not least the Les Paul electrics which had come back into fashion during the late 1960s. Seth Lover found that his new employers effectively wanted an exact soundalike copy of a Gibson humbucking pickup. No surprise there.

The patent had not quite run out, so Lover designed for Fender a pickup that looked slightly different – it had staggered sets of three poles visible on the cover, as opposed to the straight line of six poles seen on a Gibson cover. Lover also took into account Fender's inclination to a brighter sound by keeping a little more brilliance in the Fender pickup's tone than there was in the Gibson.

Another new recipient of the Fender humbucker was the Telecaster Deluxe of 1973. This seemed like a cross between the big-headstocked neck and the vibrato of a Strat, the body of a Tele, and the pickups and controls of a Gibson. Potential customers were generally confused, and stayed away from the Deluxe. But they certainly did not stay away from many of Fender's other models. Marketing director David Gupton announced that 1972 had been a record year for Fender, with unit production and dollar sales figures both higher than ever before. He was in little doubt that 1973 would be higher still, and that the trend would continue upward. A major expansion program was on at the Fullerton plant to boost output still further.

This is precisely why CBS had purchased Fender back in 1965. But the increase in instruments leaving the factory inevitably affected quality. A feeling was beginning to set in that Fenders were not made like they used to be. This coupled with a number of top musicians regularly seen playing old guitars – now described as "vintage" instruments – added to the growing impression that numbers might be more important to Fender than quality.

The world's favorite recording machine

This Telecaster Deluxe was made about 1976.

Lowell George (right) of Little Feat was a remarkably gifted guitarist, and a keen Strat man. The band's Dixie Chicken LP was out this year.

The promo department decided to stress the favoritism afforded Fenders in a new series of cartoon-inspired ads.

Listening to records is real pleasure. Making records is all business. Everything rides on the sound, and more professionals choose the "Fender Sound"... controlled distortion or pure clean projection. Listen to your favorite record. Chances are it was cut using Fender.® Fender amps are the number one selling amps in the world. For business and pleasure, turn on to Fender... guitars and amps that are made for each other.

Fender
CBS Musical Instruments

1974
Slap that bass

Production lines were still jammed on full throttle, churning out hundreds of instruments a day. They fell into some talented hands, few more exciting than those of Larry Graham (left). The ex-Sly & The Family Stone bassman defined slap funk on his Jazz Bass, and formed Graham Central Station, whose startling first album (right) was out this year.

The catalog of guitars and basses was by 1974 beginning to settle down to a revised pattern. After the cold reception for the recent spate of "new" humbucker-equipped models, Fender's taste for fresh designs slackened off considerably.

A glance at the chronology assembled at the rear of this book tells its own story about the singular lack of new models in the 1970s. It's clear that Fender was quite sensibly concentrating in general on its strengths – and as a result was enjoying its most successful period, producing a greater quantity of instruments than it had ever done in its entire history.

Remaining at the top of the line for solidbody electrics was the Jaguar, at $460 in sunburst, closely followed by the Jazzmaster at $430. Strats came with various specs including maple neck, "hardtail" (no vibrato), and left-handed choices, with the regular rosewood-fingerboard sunburst model priced at $380. A further $18 would secure you a Custom Color Strat, now down to a sorry list of blond, white, black, natural, or walnut. Custom Colors were discontinued altogether this year for Jag and Jazzmaster. You could have sunburst or sunburst, to misquote Henry Ford. No doubt Henry would have been impressed by the mass-production on display at Fullerton.

As you continued to glance at the pricelist so thoughtfully tucked into your 1970s catalog, you'd notice that Telecasters came in a similar array of specs such as maple neck and left-handers, and also with a

Bigsby vibrato option. However, a regular rosewood-'board blond Tele was pitched at $295, plus $15 if you could find a Custom Color that took your fancy. The basic Tele Deluxe in Walnut was $410; the Tele Custom $325; and Tele Thinline $385. Three budget guitars completed the line: the $229 Mustang, $189 Bronco, and $172 Musicmaster. The bass list was headed by the Jazz, with maple neck or left-hand options, retailing at $366 for the standard rosewood-fingerboard model (plus $18 for Custom Color: blond, white, black, natural, or walnut). The Telecaster Bass was still there, at $312 for a blond, followed by the Precision in quite a number of options including maple neck, narrow neck, fretless and left-hand. The regular rosewood-board sunburst Precision Bass sold for $305, plus $14 for the same limited set of Custom Colors as the Jazz. Rounding off the bass catalog was the Bass VI at $387, Mustang for $249, and Musicmaster at $149.

One more sign of the vastly increased production at Fender was the cessation of neck dates. Since the earliest days of Esquires and Broadcasters, workers had almost always pencilled and later rubber-stamped dates on the body-end of necks. It's about the most reliable way to date a Fender – leaving aside the question of fakes. But from 1973 to the early 1980s Fender stopped doing it. Too busy, presumably.

Proto-funk band The Meters relied on the solid groove of Fender-fancying guitarist Leo Nocentelli.

MEANWHILE IN 1974...

PATTY HEARST, daughter of publisher Randolph Hearst, is kidnapped by the Symbionese Liberation Army.

DARWIN, AUSTRALIA devastated by Cyclone Tracy.

WHITE HOUSE tapes subpoenaed in Watergate hearings. Nixon is impeached, and resigns – first US president to do so. Gerald Ford sworn in; grants full pardon to Nixon.

GREEK junta collapses; first elections held since 1967.

BARCODES introduced for product pricing. The first item sold using a barcode is a pack of Wrigley's chewing gum.

ALEXANDER SOLZHENITSYN is deported to the West.

This Jazz Bass was made around 1977. The model had been available with the option of a maple neck and block "pearl" markers since the late 1960s, but it was in the 1970s and later that a number of funk and jazz players began to favor this version, including Larry Graham and Marcus Miller. The Jazz Bass pictured has the "bullet" truss-rod adjuster and three-bolt neck fixing introduced to the model in 1975.

Speed, decided Fender's ever-busy promo people, was of the essence in this new series of ads.

Bronze metal

Fender's instruments were being sold in over 3,000 music stores throughout the world, and in the US alone there were 19 salesmen dedicated to Fender promotion. Leo Fender was long gone from the company, but his name was being used on a vast number of products ranging from Leo's original lines – steel guitars and amplifiers – to PA equipment, electric pianos and, of course, electric guitars.

The UK distributor of Fender was CBS/Arbiter, a joint venture formed with Ivor Arbiter who had been the company's British agent since the mid 1960s when he'd taken over from Jennings and Selmer. Arbiter had opened the Fender Soundhouse, a new instrument superstore in London's Tottenham Court Road, toward the end of 1973.

Sculptor Jon Douglas had been working at Arbiter's house, and was invited to visit the store. When he noted that most of the guitars looked "boring," Arbiter invited him to do better. Douglas came up with a replacement Stratocaster body made from cold-cast bronze, employing a metallic layer over a fiberglass shell. A prototype (pictured opposite) was made, followed by six more models. Each had the sculpted body, in a variety of shades, and after a suggestion from Arbiter rhinestones were set into the body's surface, providing the instrument's name. This small batch of Rhinestone Stratocasters was put on sale at the Soundhouse in 1975, but unfortunately a fire destroyed the premises soon afterwards. It would seem that two of the "production" models had already been sold, but the other four are likely to have perished in the flames. Douglas made fresh molds for a further run of around 25 examples in the early 1990s, some

adapting old 1970s parts, others with modern components, and all identified by a numbered plaque set into the molding on the rear of the body.

As 1970s Stratocasters with replacement bodies, original Rhinestone Strats might fail to excite "vintage" collectors. But the connection with Jon Douglas, who continued to work as a sculptor before his death in the 1990s, certainly make them significant as the first Fender "art" guitars.

Over in California, not much was changing in the Fender lines. A little fiddling was done to the budget-price Musicmaster guitar, and the Jazz Bass was brought into line with the other models that had adopted the tilt-neck system, "bullet" truss-rod adjuster at the headstock, and three-bolt neck fixing.

Musical highlights from Fender men included Bruce Springsteen's *Born To Run* album, with Springsteen memorably pictured clutching his trusty Esquire on the inner sleeve (top of page) alongside saxophonist Clarence Clemons. Springsteen's lead guitarist, Miami Steve Van Zandt, was often seen with a Strat, as was Nils Lofgren, who would join Springsteen's band in later years. Lofgren's first solo album (left) showcased the ex-Neil Young musician as a talented composer and incisive guitarist.

This Rhinestone Stratocaster prototype was made in 1975.

Aston Barrett (below) was the brilliant Jazz-toting bassman in Bob Marley's Wailers. The band's fine Live! and Natty Dread LPs were out this year.

Fairy tales (left) were the next source of inspiration for Fender's continuing ad series. "If everyone minded their own business," said the Duchess in a hoarse growl, "the world would go round a deal faster than it does."

© 1975 CBS Inc

-fo-fum!" bellowed the
as Jack streaked for the bean-
stalk. "Bring back the treasures you
ripped off or I'll grind your bones to
make my bread."
 "From now on," taunted Jack,
cradling the stolen Precision Bass in

when I lay down some licks on your
electric bass."
 "On my *Fender* electric bass!"
moaned the Giant. "Anything but the
best isn't worth a hill of beans. When
you get to the root of the matter,

For a full-color poster of this ad, send $1 to:
Fender, Box 3410, Dept. 375, Fullerton, CA 92634.

Source: National Marketing Research of California, 1975.

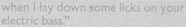

Casting the star

The guitar R&D department broke a three-year silence to introduce a new model, the hollowbody Starcaster, but it still failed to improve the company's performance alongside Gibson's hollowbody electrics, and the model was gone from the catalog in less than four years. New pedal-steels (right) included Artist and Student models. The most notable players forging ahead with Fender this year were Jeff Beck (above) and Jaco Pastorius (below).

© 1976 CBS Inc.

The Starcaster was another attempt to lure guitarists away from their Gibson thinline hollowbody electrics. Launched in 1976, it was a much better instrument than some of the previous hollowbody models, but still failed to excite players. The project started life as another of CBS's attempts to use old stock, as they had done with the previous Custom and Swinger.

But early prototypes were too obviously outings for scrap components from Coronados, so management gave designer Gene Fields the go-ahead to come up with a completely new guitar. The result was a hollowbody electric more in keeping with Fender's overall style, bearing an offset-waist body and a Fender-like headstock.

Despite the inherent quality of the $850 Starcaster, its timing was wrong, and most potential customers still opted for Gibson hollowbody models. Later on, Fender decided not to waste valuable Strat and Tele production time on the Starcaster, and the guitar had left the list by 1980.

The new Super Twin amp marked the high point of a trend towards power: it produced no less than 180 watts from within a regular-size 2x12 combo cabinet. Visually the model was in contrast to the "silverface" look prevalent at Fender at the time, and adopted a

black control panel that hinted at the old (and today revered) "blackface" style. The new amp had done well in the laboratory, but never managed to attract many real-world players to its fulsome charms.

Jeff Beck had gone back to using a Gibson Les Paul for his acclaimed 1975 jazz-rock album *Blow By Blow*, but for the fine follow-up *Wired* (top of page) the guitarist took up Strats once more – and has stayed faithful on almost every recording since.

Another influential Fender player was Jaco Pastorius, whose astonishing solo album (left) came out this year. Pastorius popularized the sound of fretless bass, playing his de-fretted Jazz Bass (as well as a regular fretted Jazz) in a virtuosic manner as a featured instrument. The album included the double-tracked 'Continuum' that defined the Jaco fretless sound. A year later Pastorius would join the jazz-rock group Weather Report, with whom he stayed for six eventful years, further enhancing the appeal of the fretless.

Fender's serial-numbering system changed this year to the style still used today. From 1976, the first two characters of most serials indicate the approximate year of manufacture. An opening letter defines the decade – S for 1970s, E for 1980s, N for 1990s, and T for 2000s – and the number following it fixes the year. Thus N6149736 indicates 1996. It's not 100 per cent accurate, and there are anomalies, but it offers a reasonable guide to production period.

Fender had used the Tarrega brandname for some classical guitars in the 1960s, but by now (right) it was for strings.

This Starcaster was made around 1978.

He's a child of science. He's a child of music. And he lives in every Fender.

The Starmaker. He's the spirit in every Fender guitar, bass and amplifier that turns mild-mannered brothers and sisters into hand-clapping, foot-stomping hordes. And turns recording tape into gold.

The Starmaker. He's the

This year's ads (right) had Fender products frightening the wildlife.

humbucking pick-ups that yield an incredibly wide frequency response so you can play anything from rock, country and soul. Create just the right pieces that are magnets from head to thread (Not magnetized screws.) Shielded all Starcasters' cables with braided wire to cut hum off where it starts. And added a solid center block—molded and flushed to the back and top of the guitar—for more sustain.

Staying with the earlier fairy-tale ad theme, Snow White and the Witch (left) get down to a Starcaster-led groove.

The Starcaster. It's a sound at home in New York, Nashville or Detroit. An instrument built to meet all the demands of the studio, stage and road. And the reason to fly down to your authorized Fender dealer.

Because your flight to the Stars starts with Fender.

The production onslaught at the Fullerton factories was designed to supply a demand for Fender guitars and amps across a wide range of musical tastes – a range that Fender hinted at in its amusing sartorially-diverse ad of 1977 (left). Dressing up the guitars themselves seemed less likely, although the revived Antigua shaded finish did at least bring some brightness to a depleted list of Custom Colors.

A shortlived revival began this year of the Antigua finish, the light-to-dark shaded color that had first been offered as an option during the late 1960s on some of the Coronado models. Back then, the finish had been adopted as an emergency measure to disguise manufacturing flaws. But this time around it was deployed purely for its aesthetic appeal.

Fender's list of Custom Colors had been pared right back, and the new-style Antigua at least offered some brightness among a somewhat dowdy list of around half a dozen options. Models available in Antigua were the standard Strat and Tele, plus the Telecaster Deluxe and Custom, the Mustang and Mustang Bass, and the Jazz and Precision Bass. This new Antigua style, now with more of a graduated tone, was matched to similarly finished pickguards.

Also featured on the new Antigua guitars was the new black hardware that Fender had started to use from 1975. All the plasticware – knobs, pickup covers, switch caps and all – was now black, and this certainly enhanced the overall look of the Antigua-finish instruments. It was also around this time that Fender's tuners were generally replaced by closed-cover units bought in from the German Schaller company, a supplier used until 1983.

Cut-backs in the electric guitar line had been continuing: the Duo-Sonic had been dropped in 1969; the last Esquire of the period was made in 1970; and the Jaguar had disappeared around 1975. On the Stratocaster, Fender began to fit a five-way selector switch from 1977, replacing the old three-way unit.

From its launch in 1954 the Strat bore a selector pickup switch that offered three firm settings: neck pickup, or middle pickup, or bridge pickup. Later, some players began to discover that if the switch was lodged precariously between the "official" settings, combinations of pickups became available.

Lodging the three-way switch between neck and middle settings gave those two pickups combined, and similarly for middle and bridge. There was also a change to the quality of the sound in these in-between positions, caused by phase cancellation and producing "hollow" or "honky" sounds – as well as a volume decrease – that could be quite useful musically.

Players would sometimes loosen the spring inside the switch to make it easier to lodge the switch at in-between settings. Some accessory manufacturers spotted the trend and began to offer replacement five-way switches that gave the standard three positions plus two firm, "clickable" settings for the new sounds. It took Fender until 1977 to change the standard switch on the Stratocaster to a five-way unit. The guitarist probably most identified with the "hollowed-out" sounds of the inbetweenies was Mark Knopfler of Dire Straits, whose debut album of 1978 would be awash with the sounds of phase-cancelled Strat pickups.

Television's debut album (below) appeared this year, with Tom Verlaine's brilliant Jazzmaster work to the fore.

This Mustang Bass (main guitar) in Antigua was made around 1978, as was the Antigua-finish Strat (right).

Tele master Roy Buchanan is pictured with his main squeeze on this 1977 LP.

1978
Lost in music

At the Fender factories, hundreds of new guitars were being packed for shipping every day. They became the raw material for musicians intent on discovering yet more ways of broadening the scope of pop music. Punk was becoming new wave. Dance music had fractured into disco, funk and soul. And rock was facing an identity crisis, forced to adopt parallel roles as jazz-rock, country-rock, heavy-rock, and more.

To survey key Fender players during the late 1970s is to underline the sheer diversity of popular music at the time. Some of it was startlingly good, some embarrassingly bad, some simply pathetic. But the fan of the time could hardly complain about lack of choice. Guitarists were worried that the newly popular keyboard synthesizer might devalue and even eclipse the electric guitar in pop, but eventually it settled alongside the other instruments. Although the sonic possibilities for the guitar were now virtually limitless with modern amps and effects, Fender's traditionally bright sound was well positioned to cut through a band that might now include synths and drum machines as much as the more usual components.

Guitar® PLAYER

Some great debut albums appeared this year: The Police (above) had Andy Summers on a Tele, Sting on Precision; Dire Straits meant Mark Knopfler (opposite, top left) and a cleanly flowing Strat; while Chic's Nile Rodgers (opposite, top right) often used a Strat for his insistent, irresistible grooves.

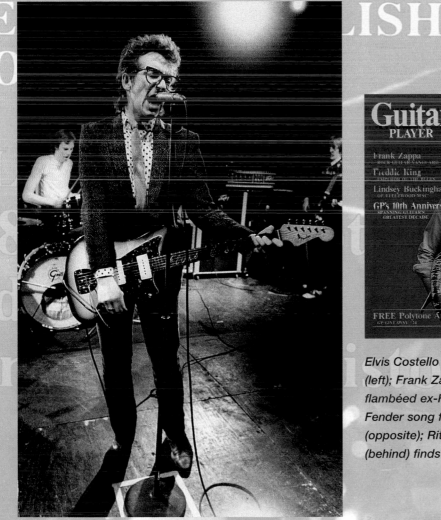

Elvis Costello with Jazzmaster (left); Frank Zappa (above) and flambéed ex-Hendrix Strat; an all-Fender song for Talking Heads (opposite); Ritchie Blackmore (behind) finds #11 on his Strat.

1979

Anniversary schmaltz

As the 1970s came to a close, the first Fender anniversary model appeared, intended to mark 25 years of the Stratocaster. There was little beyond the dated neckplate on the back of the body to connect the instrument with the mid 1950s. It was almost as if CBS was underlining the fact that Fender back then was a whole world away from the modern operation. Down at the bottom of the pricelist, two new budget Lead models made a brief appearance.

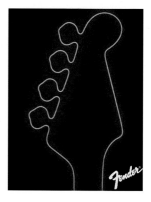

This year marked the 25th anniversary of the introduction of the Stratocaster, and Fender decided to celebrate the occasion with its first-ever anniversary model. Today, we might expect a nit-picking replica accurate enough to satisfy the most anal of collectors. Not so in 1979.

About the only concessions to the design specifics of a 1954 Strat were the fretted maple neck and body-end truss-rod adjustment. Otherwise what you got was a 1979 Stratocaster with a unique paint job, a cheesy ANNIVERSARY logo on the upper horn, a celebratory neck-plate with special serial number, and locking Sperzel tuners.

Fender had shifted during 1979 from its multi-coat "thick skin" polyester finish to a water-based paint. The earliest examples of the 25th Anniversary Strat used the new finish, in Pearl White. Unfortunately this cracked spectacularly. Most were sent back to the factory from irate stores or owners, and Fender reverted to polyester paints. The main production of the 25th Anniversary was changed to a more appropriate silver finish.

"The quantity, naturally, is limited," announced Fender... who during 1979 and 1980 proceeded to make thousands of 25th Anniversary Stratocasters ($800 including case, virtually the same price as a standard model). "They went fast in '54. They'll go fast now," ran the insistent ad. An official estimate of production mentioned some 10,000 units.

The model 75 amp came out this year, incorporating some influences from the MESA Boogie amps that had been causing a stir at the time. Boogies had popularized master volume controls for more precise overdrive/distortion control, and channel switching for selecting between clean and overdrive channels with a footswitch. Fender's 75 adopted these features, as well as some technical trickery to provide overdrive at a switchable lower power.

Gregg Wilson in R&D landed the job of designing a new pair of "student" models, intended eventually to replace the Musicmaster, Bronco, and Mustang that sat at the bottom of the company's six-string pricelist at the time. Wilson's new guitars were the Lead I and Lead II, introduced in 1979. They were simple, double-cutaway solidbodies, but ended up not especially cheap at $399. For the time being, the original budget trio remained: the Mustang retailing for $450, the Bronco $340, and the Musicmaster $320 (all these prices including a case). John Page, whom we'll meet again later, designed a variation, the Lead III of 1981, but none of the Lead guitars lasted beyond 1982.

Apparently there was a joke often heard around Fender at the time: "We don't build them like we used to... and we never did." CBS was selling 40,000 Fender instruments a year by the end of the 1970s.

The two-humbucker Lead III (right) completed the shortlived Lead line in 1981.

MEANWHILE IN 1979...

THREE MILE ISLAND nuclear plant in Pennsylvania declares emergency as radiation leaks after partial meltdown.

THE MUPPET MOVIE increases the size of key players Kermit The Frog and Miss Piggy.

EARL MOUNTBATTEN (along with three others) and British MP Airey Neave are murdered in separate attacks by IRA.

MOBILE PHONES in first commercial network in Tokyo.

SHAH leaves Iran; Muslim leader Ayatollah Khomeini returns from exile, executing pro-Shah generals. Students occupy US embassy; President Carter stops Iran oil imports.

New budget Lead I and Lead II models seen in a 1979 catalog (below). A Lead Bass (right) was planned but never reached production.

This 25th Anniversary Stratocaster was manufactured in 1979.

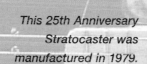

Robert Smith of The Cure (right) is a long-time Jazzmaster fan. The band's debut LP appeared this year.

● *Blond Telecaster, Rosewood Fingerboard,1979 retail price: $645.00, equivalent in today's money: $1,520, value of 1979 example now: $1,000*

"Diversification was the key to this Fender decade, with fresh models, Japanese production, signature guitars, and a new Custom Shop."

Signs appeared of a realization that some Fenders might be out of touch with current trends. The Stratocaster and the Precision Bass were given a makeover, creating alongside the regular models the new Precision Special Bass (right) and Strat. Quite happy with the existing fare was Iron Maiden (Dave Murray, Stratocaster, and Steve Harris, P-bass, left), architects of heavy rock with a debut LP out this year.

Most people tend to refer to a Stratocaster as a "Strat," and in 1980 Fender finally used the abbreviation officially on a new model designed by Gregg Wilson. It was Wilson who had come up with the budget Lead models, introduced the previous year.

Fender's new Strat combined standard Stratocaster looks with updated circuitry, a "hot" bridge pickup, and fashionable, heavy-duty brass hardware. The latter was also offered by Fender as Original Brass Works after-market accessories, following the lead of various companies who had popularized a craze for retrofit replacement parts. Larry DiMarzio had been in the forefront of this new business, introducing his Super Distortion replacement pickup in 1975, with Mighty Mite, Seymour Duncan and others following soon.

Fender also intended with the Strat to re-introduce the old-style narrow headstock of the original Stratocasters – the larger type of the time had been in use since around 1965 – but as old worn-out tooling was used the result was not an entirely accurate re-creation. Smaller, certainly; accurate, no. A reversion to the four-bolt neck fixing, body-end truss-rod adjustment, and removal of the neck-tilt for the new Strat also implied that CBS were already aware of criticisms of 1970s Stratocasters.

A few brighter colors were offered for the Strat, too, reviving Lake Placid Blue, Candy Apple Red, and Olympic White. The Strat retailed at $995, compared to $745 for a regular Stratocaster of the time. A similar

makeover provided a new option to the regular Precision, the Precision Special Bass. Brass hardware, body-end truss-rod adjuster, brighter colors and the rest were there, plus a switchable active circuit. Again, this indicated that CBS had an eye on current trends.

Active electronics meant wider tonal potential thanks to an on-board pre-amp. The bassist was able to boost treble and bass tones on an active bass, whereas normal "passive" circuits can only cut from existing tones. California maker Alembic had done much to publicize active basses during the 1970s, but probably more galling for CBS was Leo Fender's superb active bass guitar, the StingRay, launched by his new Music Man operation in 1976. Both the Strat and Precision Special would last in the Fender line until 1983.

One further attempt this year to provide something different for Stratocaster fans was the Hendrix Stratocaster, which turned out to be a very limited run indeed. This was something like a 25th Anniversary Strat in overall spec, but with an inverted headstock and additional body contouring, and only in white. It's significant as the first Fender made to highlight an association with a musician – a sales technique that would become very important to the company from the late 1980s – but only 25 or so were actually produced.

This Strat in Lake Placid Blue was made in 1980.

The new Strat in two promo items: a 1980 ad (below) and a 1981 catalog that – despite Fender's captions – shows a Stratocaster, a Strat, and a Stratocaster, top to bottom.

1981
In with the new

A turning point occurred as new management was installed by CBS. The owners had clearly been rattled by Fender's tendency to follow rather than lead instrument fashions. New men from Yamaha's US operation were hired, and changes were felt relatively quickly as a new-spec Stratocaster Standard was launched.

CBS management decided that new blood was needed to help reverse the decline in Fender's image. Income had been climbing spectacularly to 1980, tripling in that year compared to 1971's $20million revenues, but re-investment was wavering.

During 1981 key personnel were recruited from the US-based instrument arm of the giant Japanese company Yamaha. John McLaren was brought in to head up CBS Musical Instruments overall, Bill Schultz was the new Fender president, and Dan Smith was director of marketing, electric guitars. Schultz was given the go-ahead by CBS to try to improve matters.

Briefly available was a new set of Custom Colors known as International Colors, illustrated in the 1981 catalog (above left), intended to make existing stock more attractive. However, many of the hues were distinctly lurid – as indicated by the Capri Orange Stratocaster pictured (above), alongside a more reserved Sahara Taupe model. They were not liked at the time. (The Sahara Taupe Stratocaster shown is an oddity in itself as the neck has a four-screw fixing and no "bullet" on the large headstock, indicating it may originally have been intended for a 25th Anniversary.)

One of the first changes Dan Smith made was to revise the Strat's overall specs, introducing the Stratocaster Standard as the new regular model. It reverted to body-end truss-rod adjustment, a revamped narrow headstock shape, and what was generally felt to be the more stable four-screw neck/body fixing. (The

cover of the 1981 catalog – pictured above – was printed before the changes and shows the earlier "large" headstock.) Schultz recommended a large investment package, primarily aimed at modernizing the factory. This had the immediate effect of virtually stopping production while new machinery was brought in and staff was re-trained.

John Page in R&D provided the next generation of budget-price solidbodies with 1981's single-cutaway Bullet series. The Bronco and Musicmaster had been dropped in 1980, the Mustang in 1981. Fender decided for the first time in its history to shift manufacturing outside the United States, aiming to eliminate tooling costs. Joining a general trend in the early 1980s among many guitar companies both Western and Eastern, Fender decided to try Korean manufacturing. But early samples were poor, and Fender decided not to have the Bullets made entirely in Korea.

At first Bullets were assembled in the US with Korean parts, but even this method failed to produce guitars of a high enough standard. By late 1981 the Bullets were back to full American production, and Fender's first experience of oriental manufacturing was over. The Bullets lasted until 1983, in which year various shortlived double-cutaway versions were also produced.

This Bullet was produced around 1982.

Adrian Belew, known for deploying modified Strats and Mustangs to devastating effect, was in fine form on King Crimson's densely-textured *Discipline* (above).

Two Bullet ads here: for the shortlived double-cutaway Fender Bullet (right) and the later Squier Bullets, begun in 1983 (far right).

THE SOUND THAT CREATES LEGENDS

Japanese production began this year, and the first Vintage reissues were out, recreating classic models with 1950s and 1960s period styling. The 1982 catalog (above) stressed the heritage with cover stars from Holly to Hendrix. Plenty of current stars still rated Fender too, while some aligned with other brands – such as the Rickenbacker-inclined Tom Petty (right) – often made space for a Fender.

By the dawn of the 1980s the US dollar had soared in value relative to the Japanese yen. Coupled with the high quality of many guitars being exported from dozens of increasingly skilled Japanese manufacturers, this meant that lots of players were cheerfully ignoring American-made guitars and opting for well-made, good-price instruments made in the orient.

A good deal of these instruments were copies of the Fender Stratocaster, which was enjoying renewed popularity. And the Japanese copyists were making the biggest profits in their own domestic market. So the new Fender management team looked hard at the market, and figured that the best place to hit back at them was in Japan – by making and selling guitars there. Fender would, in effect, copy itself.

So it was that negotiations began with two Japanese instrument distributors, Kanda Shokai and Yamano Music, to establish the Fender Japan company. The joint venture was officially established in March 1982. After discussions with Tokai, Kawai, and other manufacturers, the factory chosen to build guitars for Fender Japan was Fujigen. The plant was based in Matsumoto, some 130 miles north-west of Tokyo. Fujigen was best known in the West for the excellence of its Ibanez-brand instruments.

Back at Fender HQ, another part of the plan emerged. Fender would recreate the guitars that many players and collectors were spending large sums of money to acquire: the "vintage" guitars made back in

the company's glory years in the 1950s and 1960s. The Vintage reissue series began in 1982. The guitars consisted of a maple-neck '57 Stratocaster and '57 Precision Bass, a rosewood-fingerboard '62 Strat and '62 Precision, a '62 Jazz Bass, and a '52 Telecaster.

Aside from some die-hard Fender collectors, most people who saw the new guitars praised and welcomed them. Production of the Vintage models was planned to start in 1982 at Fender US (Fullerton) and Fender Japan (Fujigen), but changes being instituted at the American factory meant that the US versions did not come on-stream until early 1983.

Fender Japan's guitars at this stage were being made only for the internal Japanese market, but one of Fender's European agents was pressing for budget-price models to compete with other Japanese imports. So Fender Japan made some less costly versions of the Vintage reissues for European distribution, starting in 1982. These were distinguished at first by a small Squier Series logo on the tip of the headstock. This was soon changed, with a large Squier marque replacing the Fender logo.

Thus the Squier brand was born. The name came from a string-making company, V.C. Squier, that Fender had acquired in 1965. Victor Carroll Squier had founded his firm in 1890 in Battle Creek, Michigan. The Squier name would become increasingly valuable to Fender in the coming years.

A Vintage '52 Telecaster (above) pictured in Fender's 1982 catalog.

MEANWHILE IN 1982...

ARGENTINA invades Falkland Islands. Britain recaptures its Crown Colony after horrifying military encounters.

PALESTINIANS massacred in West Beirut refugee camps by Lebanese Christian Phalangists.

30,000 WOMEN ring the perimeter of the UK's Greenham Common military base in an anti nuclear-missile protest.

AIDS, acquired immune deficiency syndrome, is named. A year later its cause is clear: the human immuno-deficiency virus, or HIV, which by 1999 had some 30 million carriers.

CD PLAYERS are introduced by CBS/Sony and Philips.

An ad from the late 1960s (below left) uses Jimi Hendrix to promote Esquier strings, made by the Fender-owned Squier company. The Squier name was revived by Fender in 1982 for a new line of Japanese-built guitars. This Squier Series Stratocaster (below) was made in 1982.

This Squier Series '62 Jazz Bass — note the regular Fender logo – was produced in 1982.

Another model from the Vintage series pictured in Fender's 1982 catalog, this is a '57 Precision Bass (left).

STANDARD		
1 single-coil lead		
1 single-coil rhythm		
1 volume, 1 tone		
lead/both/rhythm		

Elite complications

Change was still clearly detectable in the air this year as the Japanese-made Squier-brand guitars first went on sale in the US (ad, right), and the American-made Vintage models finally began to come off the production line ('57 Strat, bottom left). A new high-end line known as the Elite Series was launched, Paul Rivera's new take on solid-state amps (London/Montreux/Showman) appeared... and Eric Clapton borrowed a Strat from Salvador Dali (above left).

The Japanese-made Squier series, introduced in 1982 and now with a large Squier logo, was put on sale this year in America. The first US Squier ad to appear (above right) majors on the Vintage Tele, Strat and P-Bass. This marked the start of the sale of Fender Japan products around the world, and the move by Fender to become an international manufacturer of guitars. It taught the new team at Fender an important lesson, and one that earlier managements would not have believed: that musicians would buy Fender guitars with "made in Japan" on them.

At one time there had certainly been a resistance by many players to the cheap image associated with Japanese-made guitars. But the rise in quality of the instruments from brands such as Ibanez, Yamaha, Fernandes, Aria, Tokai – and Fender and Squier – wiped away a good deal of this prejudice. Oriental guitars were gaining a new popularity and respectability. At the US factory this year some cost-cutting changes were made to the Standard models. The alterations were the result of the dollar's strength and the consequent difficulty in selling US-made products overseas, where they were becoming increasingly high-priced. Savings had to be made, so the Strat lost a tone control and its distinctive jack plate, while the Tele shed its tone-enhancing through-body stringing. Minor mods were also made to the Standard basses. The revisions to the six-strings were ill-conceived, and many who had applauded the improvements made since 1981 groaned inwardly at the familiar signs of economics once again apparently taking precedence over playability and sound. Fortunately, these mutant varieties of Fender's key models lasted only until 1985.

Another shortlived series from the same period consisted of the Elite Stratocaster, Elite Telecaster, and Elite Precision Bass. These were radical new high-end versions of the old faithfuls. But the vibrato-equipped Elite Strat came saddled with a terrible bridge, which is what most players recall when the Elites are mentioned. In-fighting at Fender had led to last-minute changes and the result was an unwieldy, unworkable piece of hardware.

The Elite Strat also featured three pushbuttons for pickup selection, not to the taste of players brought up on the classic Fender switch. There were good points – the new pickups, the effective active circuitry, and the improved truss-rod design – but they tended to be overlooked. The Elites – including optional gold-hardware and walnut neck/body versions – were dropped by 1985.

This Gold Elite Telecaster in Emerald Green was produced during 1983.

MEANWHILE IN 1983...

SUICIDE BOMBERS kill 237 US marines and 58 French paratroopers in a single attack in Beirut, Lebanon.

BREAKFAST TV and new £1 coin introduced in UK.

WOODY ALLEN's *Zelig* underlines the increasing ability of film technicians to falsify historical images.

SOUTH KOREAN Boeing 747 apparently in Soviet airspace is shot down by Soviet fighter. All 269 on board are killed.

GERRY ADAMS is leader of the Irish Republican movement.

MICHAEL JACKSON's *Thriller* is released. The album is an instant bestseller, going on to sell around 45 million copies.

Cost-cutting meant the Standard Strat (right) lost its jack plate and a tone knob.

Some amps moved to oriental production too, including the rollerskating Sidekicks (above).

Closing in on the Elite Strat (left) the 1983 catalog highlighted its most criticized features: the poor vibrato bridge, and three pushbuttons in place of a pickup switch.

Turning Japanese

The new Fender Japan operation was still the main production base because the US factory's machines, systems, and staff were gradually recovering from reorganization. New models emerged from Japan – the Flame (right, top), Esprit (right, below), and D'Aquisto, plus more reissues. Further musical diversity was evident from Fender players, as Los Lobos (above) mixed rockabilly and Tex-Mex, and Johnny Marr (opposite) underpinned the melodic pop of The Smiths.

Another colorful ploy to try to use up existing stock was the "Bowling Ball" or "Marble" finish applied to 100 or so each of the Strat and Tele Standards at the US factory. The red, yellow or blue streaked effects were striking – but not really enough to detract from the shortcomings of the guitars themselves.

On the other side of the world, the new Fender Japan operation was busy adding new models to its Vintage reissue series. This time the magnifying glass was trained on a wider portion of Fender history. The earliest style of P-Bass was examined for the '51 Precision Bass; a little binding practice resulted in the '62 Custom Telecaster; and the first humbucker era was investigated to come up with the '72 Telecaster Custom and '72 Telecaster Thinline.

Three new-design lines were introduced in 1984, intended yet again to compete with some of Gibson's electric guitars. All were manufactured by Fender Japan, as Fender's US factory was still not back up to speed following the reorganizations that were being undertaken by the new management team brought in by CBS from Yamaha US.

The overall name for the new instruments was the Master Series, encompassing the electric hollowbody archtop D'Aquisto models – with design input from American luthier Jimmy D'Aquisto – and the semi-solid double-cutaway Esprit and Flame guitars.

The D'Aquistos were offered as the shortlived two-pickup Standard and the fancier single-pickup Elite.

The Elite lasted to the mid 1990s, when it moved to US manufacturing and changed to a floating pickup arrangement, alongside a new D'Aquisto Deluxe model with fixed single pickup.

The equal-cutaway Esprit and slightly-offset-cutaway Flame each came in three variations: Standard; Elite with fine-tuners; and Ultra with fine-tuners and gold-plated hardware.

Significantly for the continuing growth of Fender as an international manufacturer, these were the first Fender Japan products with the Fender rather than Squier headstock logo to be sold officially outside Japan. They were also the first ever Fender models to feature "set" glued-in necks rather than the company's customary bolt-on method, a further hint at competition with Gibson (who habitually employed set necks).

In fact, the overtly Gibson image of the Esprits and Flames was to be their undoing. Construction and quality were good; sounds and playability impressive. But they weren't "Fender." Also, Fender Japan's factory, Fujigen, had problems, and stock didn't arrive for some time. And then the owners pulled the plug. After nearly 20 years, CBS finally decided they'd had enough.

This D'Aquisto Deluxe was made in 1997.

The Smiths' first album appeared this year, with Johnny Marr (right) using classic six-strings – including a Strat – for some gloriously melodic guitar parts.

Post-CBS

CBS sold Fender to the company's management at the very start of the year, and an exciting new era for the operation was about to begin. Fenders were abundant at Live Aid, the famine-relief benefit that grabbed a global audience of 1.4billion in 170 countries, with Edge (left) a notable on-stage stylist for the impressive U2.

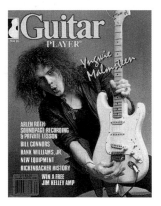

At the end of January 1985, almost exactly 20 years after acquiring it, CBS confirmed that it would sell Fender to ten "employees and foreign distributors," led by Bill Schultz. The contract for the sale was formalized in February and completed in March. The price was $12½million.

The problems Schultz and his team faced were legion. Probably the most immediate was the fact that the Fullerton factories were not included in the deal, and so US production stopped in February 1985. However, the new team had stockpiled bodies and necks, and had acquired some existing inventory of completed guitars as well as production machinery. The company went from employing some 800 people in early 1984 to just over 100 a year later.

Administration HQ was established in Brea, California, not far from Fullerton (six years later Fender moved admin from Brea to Scottsdale, Arizona), and a search began for a factory site in the general Orange County area of Los Angeles.

Fender had been working on a couple of radical guitars before the sale campaign. One was a John Page design, the Performer. It started life intended for US production, but with nowhere to build it there, manufacturing was started at Fujigen in Japan.

The Performer had a distinctive body shape, twin slanted pickups, 24 frets, and an arrow-shape headstock quite different from the usual Strat derivative. It was based on the 1969 Swinger head, to

avoid the need for a new trademark, and was a reaction to the drooped headstock of the newly prevalent "superstrat" guitars popularized by American guitar-maker Charvel/Jackson.

Despite the strengths of the thoroughly modern Performer, the model was destabilized by the turbulence from the sale. It did manage to stay in Fender's list until 1986, but it now seems a pity that such a brave guitar should have been dropped for reasons largely unconnected with the instrument itself.

Of less interest was the Katana, a response to another fashion of the time among guitar makers: the weird body shape. Dealers had pressured Fender for an odd-shape guitar, but players resisted the styling and the imposed Japanese origin of the Katana, and it too limped on only until 1986.

The Japanese operation became Fender's lifeline, providing much-needed product to a company that still had no US factory. Around 80 per cent of the guitars that Fender US sold from late 1984 to mid 1986 were made in Japan. All the guitars in Fender's 1985 catalog were made in Japan, including the new Contemporary Stratocasters and Contemporary Telecasters. These were the first relatively conventional Fenders to feature the increasingly fashionable heavy-duty vibrato systems and string-clamps made popular on superstrats.

Some of the color options (right) in Fender Japan's 1985 catalog.

509	Candy apple red (metallic).
543	Pewter (metallic).
555	Frost white (metallic).
564	Montego black (metallic).
567	Emerald mist (metallic).
566	Burgundy mist (metallic).
568	Gun metal blue (metallic).

MEANWHILE IN 1985...

MIKHAIL GORBACHEV is the new Soviet leader. Tears For Fears release 'Everybody Wants To Rule The World.'
WHAM! becomes first Western pop group to play in China.
TITANIC WRECK, sunk since 1912, found by Robert Ballard's remote-controlled deep-sea explorer, Argo.
PLO terrorists hijack Italian cruise ship Achille Lauro with 80 on board and murder an American passenger.
MICROSOFT launch Windows operating system for IBM PC.
MICHAEL J. FOX returns to 1955 in *Back To The Future* but, inexplicably, he does not stuff the De Lorean with Strats.

This Katana (right) was made by Fender Japan in 1985.

This Performer in Emerald Mist was made in 1986.

Tele man Albert Collins (left) made the Showdown album this year with another Fender fan, Robert Cray. The debut LP from Yngwie Malmsteen (opposite, top right) also appeared, an altogether more explosive, metallic affair.

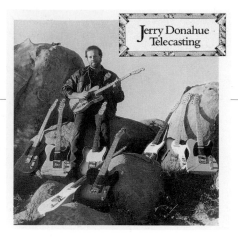

Jerry Donahue
Telecasting

Crafted in Corona

Fender's reputation among musicians was as strong as ever, with hardly a live show escaping some glimpse of the company logo – maybe on an instrument in the hands of the virtuosic Jerry Donahue (above) or Pretenders frontwoman Chrissie Hynde (right). But a plan was underway to establish straightforward, high-quality, US-made versions of the classic models: the American Standard series.

A growing number of models was being manufactured by Fender Japan for worldwide sale, as well as the instruments it made that were only available on the domestic Japanese market. Back in the United States, Fender had finally established a factory, It was at Corona, California, about 20 miles east of the now defunct Fullerton site.

Production had started at Corona on a very limited scale toward the end of 1985. At first the new factory was building only about five guitars per day for the Vintage reissue series.

The new operation had little or no money to invest in fresh tooling for brand new designs, and the team had learned from mistakes like the Elite vibrato that the focus had to be on simplicity. In general, they figured, simplicity makes things work, and does not get in the way of the player.

So it was that electric-guitar boss Dan Smith and his colleagues decided that the most advantageous way forward was to re-establish the US side of Fender's production with a good, basic Stratocaster, Telecaster, Precision Bass, and Jazz Bass. These would involve very little new costs, and would, the company hoped, be seen as a continuation of the very best of Fender's long-standing American traditions.

This general plan translated specifically into the American Standard series. The Stratocaster version was the first model to be launched, in 1986, with the Telecaster, Precision, and Jazz following on two years

later. The American Standard Stratocaster was an efficacious piece of re-interpretation. It drew from the best of the original Stratocaster, but was updated with a 22-fret neck that had a slightly flatter fingerboard, and a revised vibrato unit. The vibrato had twin knife-edge pivot points, which Fender claimed would provide increased stability, a smoother action, and much less opportunity for the number-one enemy of vibrato bridges: friction. The flat saddles, cast in stainless-steel, offered the most obvious visual clue to the presence of the new vibrato, while other technical changes allowed greater arm travel.

A new set of six color options – Arctic White, Black, Brown Sunburst, Gun Metal Blue, Pewter, and Torino Red – was made immediately available for the American Standard Strat, with changes and additions following.

Once the Corona plant's production lines reached full speed, the American Standard Strat proved to be an extremely successful model for the revitalized Fender company. By the early 1990s the guitar would be a best-seller, notching up some 25,000 sales annually. In fact in many markets today, including the United States, the various American Standard models (the "Standard" part of the name was dropped in 2000) remain firmly among the best-selling American-made Fender models.

This American Standard Stratocaster in Frost Red was made during 1991.

MEANWHILE IN 1986...

CHALLENGER space shuttle explodes 73 seconds after launch from Cape Canaveral, Florida, killing all seven crew.
REAGAN denies Iran arms-for-hostages, halts arms sales. Diversion of arms funds to Nicaraguan contras revealed.
NUCLEAR ACCIDENT at Chernobyl power station, Ukraine.
JANET JACKSON, Patti Labelle, Whitney Houston hold top US album-chart positions, a first for black or female artists.
"IT TAKES up to 40 dumb animals to make a fur coat... But only one to wear it." Respect For Animals ad slogan.
DESMOND TUTU elected Archbishop in South Africa.

The Stratocaster was joined by the American Standard Telecaster in 1988, as seen in this ad (below) from that year.

Blues-rocker Jeff Healey (right) demonstrates his unusual lap-like style on an American Standard Strat in this 1995 ad.

Jeff Healey started out on a Fender Squier. Today, The Fender US Standard Strat is an essential part of his phenomenal and unique performance.

You just know it's a *Fender*®

1987
Custom made, CA

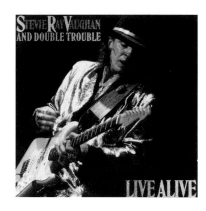

A new Custom Shop was started this year, at first making one-off artist models but gradually building a much wider role. Fender-toting musicians making waves included Stevie Ray Vaughan, whose *Live Alive* LP (right) featured blistering blues-based rock, while Thurston Moore (above) mixed noise-for-noise-sake and huge riffs to help New York band Sonic Youth turn out *Sister*, one of their finest albums yet.

In 1987 the Custom Shop was officially established at the new Corona plant so that Fender could build one-offs and special orders. While this specialist role continued – customers have ranged from Chet Atkins to Eric Johnson (below) to Lou Reed – the Custom Shop would go on to develop a much wider function within Fender's expanding business.

The Shop's activities gradually grew into three main areas. First there are the one-offs, or Master Built guitars. These are exactly what most people would understand as the work of a custom shop: instruments made by one person with acute attention to detail and a price to match. The second type is the limited edition, a special numbered run of anything from a handful to several hundred of a specific model. And third, the Custom Shop makes a general line of catalog models.

In its second year the Custom Shop produced the 40th Anniversary Telecaster, the first limited-edition production run. The limited run of 300 proved too low for the demand, so the Shop's next limited edition – the HLE (Haynes Limited Edition) Stratocaster – was upped to 500 units. Other numbered runs continued to appear from the Custom Shop and became an important part of its job. A logical extension to the limited editions

would start in 1992 with the Shop's first catalog of standard Custom Shop products. No production limit is put on these models other than the confines of the Shop's capacity.

The expansion of the Custom Shop's business prompted a move in 1993 to new buildings (but still close to the Corona factory) to gain extra space and improve efficiency, and a further move in late 1998 to Fender's new Corona plant.

An early job for the Custom Shop was to build a yellow Vintage reissue Strat for Jeff Beck. At this stage Beck vetoed Fender's wish to produce a Jeff Beck signature edition Strat, and the design intended for that purpose evolved into the Strat Plus. A Jeff Beck signature Strat not dissimilar to the Plus finally appeared in 1991.

The Strat Plus adopted a roller nut and locking tuners, fashionable features designed to improve vibrato performance. It was also the first Fender with new Lace Sensor pickups. Don Lace, an expert in magnetics, had tried to interest Fender in his designs before the CBS sale, and discussions reopened afterwards. Fender wanted to continue in the direction started with the Elite pickups, aiming for an ideal of low noise and low magnetic attraction, while still delivering the classic single-coil sound. The result was Lace Sensor pickups.

This Strat Plus in Graffiti Yellow was made in 1990.

The Custom Shop was started by John Page (above left) and John Stevens, pictured in 1987 with an early job, a Foam Green Tele Thinline for Elliot Easton of The Cars. Luthier Fred Stuart is seen at work at the Shop (left) in 1990.

Fender's US amp business was started afresh at Lake Oswego, Oregon, in 1986 under Bill Hughes. Two of the new tube models included The Twin and Dual Showman, seen in this 1987 flyer (right).

1988

Sign here please, Eric

Eric Clapton became the first musician honored with a signature edition Fender production model. He was closely followed by Yngwie Malmsteen, and many more guitarists and bassists would be similarly celebrated in the coming years. Moves were made to establish production still further afield, with some of Fender's Squier-brand instruments (catalogs, above) now coming from Korea and, briefly, India.

The first signature guitar produced by Fender was the Eric Clapton Stratocaster. In fact, the first musician with whom Fender informally discussed the possibility of a signature model had been James Burton, back in 1981, but Burton had to wait until 1990 for his signature Telecaster to appear.

Signature models have become important to the Fender line in the years since, but at first this was another bonus brought about by the new Custom Shop, which was actively pushing to pro players its services for building one-off instruments tailored to individual requirements.

Clapton asked Fender to make him a guitar that had the distinct V-shape neck of his favorite 1930s Martin acoustic guitar, as well as what he described as a "compressed" pickup sound. Various prototypes were built for Clapton by George Blanda at the Custom Shop, and the final design eventually went on sale to the public in 1988.

Fender demonstrated to Clapton that Lace Sensor pickups and a midrange-boosting active circuit could deliver the sound he was after, and curiously the production model even offers a blocked-off vintage-style vibrato unit, carefully duplicating that feature of Clapton's fave Strat (he never used vibrato, but disliked the sound of hardtail non-vibrato Strats). Clapton had retired his faithful old

"bitser" Strat, Blackie, in 1987, and started to play his new signature models soon after.

Also released in 1988 was the second signature model, the Yngwie Malmsteen Stratocaster. The most unusual aspect of the Swedish heavy metal guitarist's instrument was the scalloped fingerboard. Malmsteen claims that the absence of physical contact with the fingerboard enables him to play even faster than his already lightning technique allows. A good number of Fender signature models would follow these first two. Some were made in the Custom Shop, others came from the main factories or further afield. Each one generally bore features favored by the named artist. The company chooses its signature-model players for their contributions as musicians and their continuing involvement with Fender. "It's really more of a tribute rather than anybody getting rich," Fender's Dan Smith once explained. "The players are compensated fairly, and everybody gets the same royalty."

This year three more American Standard models – the Telecaster, the Jazz Bass, and the Precision Bass — joined the earlier Strat. The Tele was updated with a 22-fret neck and a six-saddle bridge. And the newest model from Fender Japan was the Strat XII (pictured, far left), only the second solid electric 12-string produced by Fender.

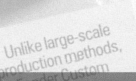

Virtually every signature model has an autograph logo on the tip of the headstock (right).

MEANWHILE IN 1988...

TERRORIST BOMB explodes on Pan-Am 747 which crashes on Lockerbie, Scotland, killing all 259 on board and 11 on the ground. Two Libyans charged in 1999, tried in 2000.

AUSTRALIA introduces first successful plastic folding money, a $10 bill marking the Australian bicentennial.

SCRIPTEL introduces a system for inputting data into a computer by writing on the screen.

CLINT EASTWOOD makes *Bird*, a film about Charlie Parker, with Forest Whitaker as the great alto saxophonist.

HOUSE and acid-house music become successful in UK.

This Eric Clapton Strat in Torino Red was made in 1990.

More vintage-flavor models were coming out, made in the US (catalog, below) and Japan, though the Blue Flower finish of this Japanese-built Strat (right) had only appeared originally on Telecasters.

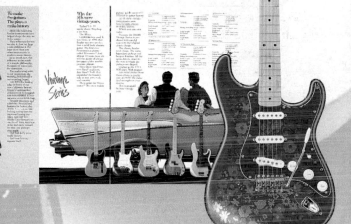

An Eric Clapton Stratocaster in Candy Green and an Yngwie Malmsteen Strat in Sonic Blue are pictured in this 1988 catalog spread (left).

The first full-blown attempt by Fender to adopt the superstrat style of guitar that had become so popular in the 1980s arrived in the shape of the HM series, out this year and made in America. Later HM models, also shortlived, included Japanese-built instruments (catalog, above, with a very unusual Fender logo, left, on that "pointy" headstock). Also in Japan, a new experimental Fender-related brand, Heartfield, was introduced.

As the 1980s drew to a close, Fender was keeping an eye carefully trained on the continuing popularity of so-called superstrat guitars. These had been developed by Charvel/Jackson, manufacturing in the US and then Japan. Subsequently, many brands such as Washburn, Ibanez, Kramer, and others adopted elements of the design in various forms.

The superstrat had started by considering a classic Stratocaster as its basis, squaring the body sides, stretching the horns, making the contouring bolder, and slimming the overall shape. The revamped body carried powerful combinations of single-coil and humbucker pickups, evolving to the preferred combination of two single-coils plus bridge humbucker.

All this was partnered by a double-locking heavy-duty fine-tunable vibrato system, meant for extreme pitch shifting. Access to the highest of the 24 frets was improved with a through-neck and deeper cutaways, and the design also popularized the drooped "pointy" headstock.

Fender's first nod toward this style had been with 1985's Performer, but this had effectively been lost in the difficulties surrounding the sale of Fender by CBS. The HM Stratocaster series, begun in 1989, tried again. This time the "HM" name was a big clue: heavy metal guitarists were the major players of such guitars,

though more mainstream guitarists such as Jeff Beck (1989 album, below left) had been briefly seduced.

Fender's HM Strats started out US-made, with most of the expected superstrat features on board, including a locking vibrato, and came with three different pickup configurations: two single-coils and a bridge humbucker; one Lace Sensor and a bridge humbucker; or two humbuckers. All were shortlived: it seemed that players generally still expected traditional Fenders from Fender.

Meanwhile the US Contemporary Stratocaster, also new in 1989, put the locking vibrato system and single/single/humbucker line-up on a conventional Strat body and neck, but this too did not last long.

A few years later Fender tried unsuccessfully again, with Japanese-made HMs (see catalog, top of page), though it wasn't really until the Floyd Rose Classic Stratocaster of 1992 that a successful blend of traditional and new features was hit upon.

Perhaps a way to avoid the un-Fender Fenders problem was to use a completely different brandname? Squier had become closely associated with Fender, so the Heartfield brand was concocted for a line of guitars considered too radical to be Fenders. They were designed by Fender US and Fender Japan and built at Fujigen in Japan. Some did have "Heartfield by Fender" logos, in a similar way to Squier, but the experiment was halted by 1993.

This double-neck Strat built in 1989 illustrates the Custom Shop's original role, making true custom instruments.

MEANWHILE IN 1989...

BERLIN WALL falls. East Germans are free to leave their country for the first time in 38 years.

HUMAN GENOME PROJECT is launched, intended to map all the genes in a human being.

3,000 STUDENTS gather in Tiananmen Square, Beijing, China, demanding political reform. Many thousands more join; martial law declared; 5,000 killed and many arrested.

AYATOLLAH KHOMEINI in Iran declares Salman Rushdie's novel *The Satanic Verses* offensive and, in a "fatwa," sentences him and his publishers to death.

Fujigen in Japan made this Fender-designed prototype (right) in 1989 as the basis for Heartfield's Talon model.

Christopher Cross (left) with another custom double-neck. Cross is best known for his 1980s hits 'Ride Like The Wind' and 'Sailing.'

"Fender was perfectly placed for the Nineties retro craze, with its glittering past continually available for re-evaluation and re-engineering."

Guitars and Basses

Albert, Danny & James

There was plenty of activity at the Fender factories this year, with new five-string bass guitars, a trio of signature models, and a reissue amp series that kicked off gloriously with a '59 tweed Bassman. In the hallowed salerooms of Sotheby's in London, another kind of history was made when a Stratocaster (pictured on the catalog, right) said to have been played by Jimi Hendrix at Woodstock was sold for the record price of £180,000 (about $270,000).

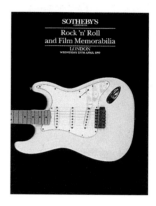

More signature model guitars appeared this year as Fender became increasingly aware of the promotional value of such instruments and "branding" was everywhere as the hip new marketing philosophy. All three of the new-for-1990 signature models were Telecasters.

Classic Texas bluesman Albert Collins was honored with a model that exchanged the neck pickup for a humbucker. Explosive technician Danny Gatton got a signature Tele with two "blade" pickups, a modified bridge, and body decoration. And former Presley sideman James Burton's model had three Strat-layout single-coils – with some bodies finished in a paisley pattern much more lurid than the guitarist's original Red Paisley Tele.

The reissue program had gone so well for guitars and basses that Fender decided to do the same for its amplifiers. The amp department had just introduced (at last!) a good new solid-state line – the M80, the RAD, the HOT, and the JAM – which had proved especially successful with younger players. Now Fender felt confident enough to delve back into the past to provide inspiration at the top of its pricelist.

The first reissue amp, out in 1990, was an obvious choice: a tweed '59 Bassman. This was almost certainly Fender's most famous amp and, despite the name, it

was a guitarist's dream. Real vintage examples had become increasingly hard to find, let alone the expense involved when one did surface. A handful of other reissues has followed, such as the "blackface" '65 Twin Reverb, and very popular they have proved.

During the 1980s a number of musicians and small bass-makers had developed the five-string bass guitar, with a low string tuned to B, and – unlike Fender's peculiar high-C Bass V – retaining the relatively wide string-spacing of a regular bass. The modern five-string bass had become an essential addition to the instruments carried by many touring and recording bassists across many styles, and by the end of the 1980s a five-string model appeared on most bass-maker's pricelists. Fender waited until 1990 to introduce its first five-string bass models. These were the Jazz Plus V (pictured, left) and the HM V. The Jazz Plus was an active-circuit Jazz Bass; the HM a three-pickup, slab-bodied heavy-rock machine.

Aside from the shortlived Esprit and Flame guitars of 1984, Fender had not strayed much from its customary bolt-on-neck construction. However, three new Set Neck Teles offered a glued joint, enabling the fashionable smooth, heel-less junction where neck meets body which some find more playable.

Danny Gatton (right) holding his original customized Tele that inspired this year's Fender signature model.

This 1990 small-run Hank Marvin signature Strat (right) predates later official versions. Please note: treating your Strat like the one on this Shadows' 1990 LP (above) is likely to put it out of warranty.

A '59 tweed Bassman led to more amp reissues, as seen in this 1993 catalog (below).

The James Burton model
"As much a James loved those stock Telecasters he used with Ricky and Elvis, they didn't give him all the sounds he wanted. So we installed three Fender-Lace® Sensors and added a five-position switch. The middle sensor sits low so as not to obstruct his picking. Now he gets those Strat sounds that you can't get from a Tele. The neck still has that same vintage feel and headstock cut, so that he can bend strings behind the nut."
George Blanda

This James Burton Telecaster in Black With Gold Paisley was made in 1991. The catalog close-up (right) shows Burton with a Frost Red example.

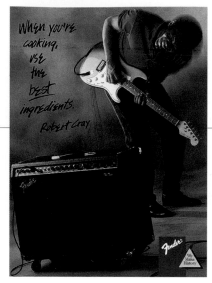

Down Mexico way

A new Fender factory based just over the California border in Mexico had been making amplifiers and cabinets for a few years, but during 1991 its first guitar products became evident, including the Standard Strat, Tele, P-Bass and Jazz. More signature models were built at the US factory, for Robert Cray (above) and Jeff Beck, while another superstrat-style instrument came along, known as the Prodigy.

Fender US came up with a new design in 1991 called the Prodigy, another shortlived attempt to compete with superstrats and their progeny. The Prodigy had an offset-waist body with sharper horns than a Strat, the requisite two single-coils and a humbucker, and an optional locking vibrato. There was a matching bass, too.

Significantly, the Prodigy was among the first Fender guitars to receive attention at the company's new factory in Ensenada, Mexico, which had been established in 1987. Ensenada is some 180 miles south of Los Angeles and is situated just across the California/Mexico border. Fender amps started to appear from Mexico in 1989, with guitars following soon after. The factory would be entirely rebuilt in 1994 after a disastrous fire.

By early 1992 the Mexican factory was assembling around 175 Fender Standard Stratocasters per day, and by 1995 had a capacity for producing 600 instruments a day. Bodies and necks for the Made In Mexico guitars were produced at the US factory in Corona and sent down to the Mexican plant. There they were sanded, painted, buffed, and assembled with Mexican-made hardware and pickups. The factory also produced all Fender's strings. By late 1997, Mexico would be assembling around 150,000 Fender guitars a year, compared to some 85,000 at Corona, with a workforce of around 1,000 at the Mexico factory and 700 at Corona.

The chief advantage to Fender of its Mexican and some offshore production sites is the cheapness of the labor. Fender has like many Western companies searched far and wide for this expediency. In addition to continuing products from Korea, the lowest-price Squier-brand Fender guitars were by 1999 being made at two factories in China, a source the company had used since the start of the 1990s.

New models from the US factory included two signature Jeff Beck and Robert Cray Strats. The Set Neck Teles continued, with a Country Artist (far left) added in 1992.

An Associated Press wire report for 21st March marked a sad occasion: "Clarence Leo Fender, whose revolutionary Stratocaster was the guitar of choice for rock stars from Buddy Holly to Jimi Hendrix, died today. He was 82. Fender was found unconscious in his Fullerton home by his wife, Phyllis, and died on the way to hospital. Fender had suffered Parkinson's disease for decades but continued to work on guitar designs." Leo had been at his bench at his G&L company just the day before, tinkering with yet another guitar improvement.

This Prodigy II in Lake Placid Blue was produced in 1991.

Leading retailers sometimes ordered unique limited runs from the Custom Shop. Only 100 of this James Jamerson Tribute bass (number 001, right) in memory of the great Motown bassist were made for The Bass Centre in LA in 1991.

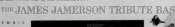

J. Mascis and his finely decorated Jazzmaster (right) were at the heart of Dinosaur Jr.'s excellent Green Mind album, out this year.

Fender Japan added a 70s Precision and a '75 Jazz Bass reissue to a Vintage line that still leaned heavily on Strats and Teles (ad, above), with the US factory contributing two more Strats, a '54 and a '60. The signature series was expanding too, resulting in this impressive ad (right) that was also made available as a handy spot-the-Fender-man poster. Bon Jovi's Richie Sambora was there, although his signature model didn't actually go on sale until 1993.

Fender's new US-made "hot" Texas Special Strat-type single-coils first appeared on this year's new Stevie Ray Vaughan signature Strat. The model had been agreed before Vaughan's tragic death in 1990 in a helicopter accident, when the guitarist's career was at full blast.

The signature model was based on Vaughan's well-used Stratocaster known as "Number One" which consisted of a basic 1959 instrument modified with a 1962 neck. Fender's Stevie Ray Vaughan Stratocaster duplicated the original instrument's substantial SRV logo on the pickguard, and also featured an unusual left-handed vibrato system, as favored by the Texas guitarist... whose work had often revealed a strong stylistic link with Jimi Hendrix.

More signature models appeared: two for Telecaster supremo Jerry Donahue – one version made in the US, the other in Japan – and for bassist Stu Hamm, who had worked with guitar virtuosi Steve Vai and Joe Satriani. Hamm's bass was the Urge, a clever blend of Jazz and Precision features that created a multi-pickup bass with wide tonal potential.

Floyd Rose, a guitar-hardware designer known for his heavy-duty locking vibrato system, joined forces with Fender late in 1991 when Fender acquired exclusive rights to Floyd Rose products. Other makers could still buy licensed hardware, but Fender seemed more interested in access to Rose's design skills, as well as the assistance that his name brought in selling guitars to the heavy metal market. To such musicians

"Floyd Rose" was almost synonymous with the heavy-duty double-locking vibrato systems so closely associated with the intense, highly-technical style of playing that peaked in the early 1990s. Fender's Floyd Rose Classic Stratocaster was launched in 1992.

The Custom Shop's "catalog" items expanded with the introduction of the American Classic Stratocaster, effectively an upscale Shop version of the factory's best-selling American Standard Strat. Several items were added to the American Classic line in coming years, including Jazz Basses and Telecasters. More unusual was the Shop's Bajo Sexto, a baritone Telecaster with a long 30" scale and a consequently deep, twangy tone.

Further from home, Korea was a new Fender production source, providing the Squier Series Standard Strat and Tele, each with regular Fender logo and small "Squier Series" on the headstock.

A year after Mike Lewis had moved to head up the amplifier marketing department, Fender's amp series was gradually remodeled into a uniform style, dumping the old "red-knob" look of recent years for something approaching classic Fender visuals. Introductions this year included the solid-state 25-watt BXR, 65-watt Deluxe 112, and 16-watt Stage 112, the hybrid 25-watt Champ 25, and the tube 60-watt Concert and 60-watt Super Amp.

US $4.95 Can $4.75 Aus $6.50

FEBRUARY 1994
UK £2.25

Plenty of Fender mayhem with Mike McCready's Strat and Stone Gossard's Jag on Pearl Jam's classic debut Ten (right).

gest and l... e guitar magazine

MEANWHILE IN 1992...

PRESIDENTS Bush and Yeltsin declare end of cold war.

BILL CLINTON elected US President.

FOUR POLICE OFFICERS acquitted of beating black suspect Rodney King in Los Angeles; violence erupts.

LARGE BOMB explodes at World Trade Center in New York.

U2 gross $64million from their US tour.

US FORCES leave the Philippines, ending nearly a century of American military presence there.

UN COUNCIL creates Bosnian "no fly zone."

SWEDEN starts first large-scale test of an AIDS vaccine.

This Stevie Ray Vaughan Strat was made in 1992.

Stu Hamm's first signature Urge Bass (right) was a keen design that merged Precision and Jazz features.

John Frusciante (right) departed the Red Hot Chilli Peppers this year after spraying some inspired Strat-fueled madness all over the Mother's Milk and Blood Sugar Sex Magik albums.

tar
mpion
s Guitar
of the Year '94

PLUS

olly Hall Real
Steve How
Pat Trave..
Bobby Mad..
Tony Arnol..
Rock Scho..

1993
Hi-ho Harley

The amp Custom Shop offered the high-end, vintage flavored Vibro-King and Tone-Master as its first products, while the existing guitar Custom Shop reflected on a 90th Anniversary Harley-Davidson Strat. Comings and goings among Fender players included an acclaimed folk-grunge debut from Liz Phair (above) and the death at 61 of the great Texas bluesman Albert Collins (memorial ad, right).

With the continuing success of the guitar Custom Shop, this year saw the start at Scottsdale, Arizona, of an amp equivalent, with ex-Matchless electronics expert Bruce Zinky in charge. The intention was to make limited quantities of expensive, high-quality products. The amp Shop would not build far-out made-to-order items, but generally would follow the guitar outfit's increasingly important business in defining a catalog of regular items.

Artists could collaborate on individually crafted items, but broadly speaking the hand-built line would be drawn from reinterpretations of Fender's classic tube amps of the 1940s, 50s and early 60s. The first models to appear from the amp Custom Shop were the Vibro-King 60-watt 3x10 combo and the Tone-Master 100-watt piggyback amp, with a choice of 2x12 or 4x12 cabinet, all finished in cream Tolex.

In the meantime at the guitar Custom Shop, over in Corona, a link was being forged with motorcycle manufacturer Harley-Davidson.

The result was the Fender Harley-Davidson 90th Anniversary Commemorative Stratocaster in a very limited run of 109 pieces. The stunning hand-engraved aluminum body summoned up the shiny exterior of a Harley, while the bird's-eye maple neck and ebony fingerboard would please anyone who actually got to play one of these creations.

The signature-guitar list continued to grow, this year with the addition of two new models, for Clarence White and Richie Sambora. The Clarence White Telecaster was named for the brilliant Byrds and Kentucky Colonels guitarist, tragically killed by a drunk driver in 1973. The White Tele was fitted with his favored Scruggs banjo-style detuners for first and sixth strings, and the B-bender string-pull device that he developed with Byrds drummer Gene Parsons.

Bon Jovi's Richie Sambora helped devise a Strat to respond to his fiery playing, with Floyd Rose double-locking vibrato, a DiMarzio bridge humbucker plus Texas Special single-coils, and a flatter, wider fingerboard. A personal touch was the inlaid stars for position markers.

On a cultural note, the Fullerton Museum Center – not far from the site of Leo Fender's original workshops – exhibited *Five Decades Of Fender*, organized by guitar historian Richard Smith. Included were instruments and memorabilia from Fender, Music Man, and G&L. Remarkably, this was the very first exhibition to feature Fender's achievements. "Leo forever changed the course of popular music," is how Smith summed it up.

G-VOX (right) was Fender's ill-fated computer teaching scheme, its special pickup linking guitar and software.

Play with it.

MEANWHILE IN 1993...

BILL MURRAY relives Groundhog Day in *Groundhog Day*.

FIRE kills 72 in Waco, Texas, after a US Federal assault on the siege taking place at a cult headquarters there.

CLINTON GALA guests include reunited Fleetwood Mac.

MOSAIC is the first software that puts the World Wide Web within the reach of most computer users.

BORIS YELTSIN's forces crush a revolt in the Russian parliament, and a new draft constitution is approved.

MAASTRICHT TREATY creates the European Union.

Fulfil your fanta...s.

Chrome... ...arilyn Monroe,... ...to yo...

In a last attempt to improve their image, the Heartfield models were rebranded Fender (below). It didn't work.

This Harley-Davidson 90th Anniversary Commemorative Strat (main guitar) was made in 1993. Another ultra-limited Custom Shop model this year was the delightful Playboy Strat, seen in the ad below.

The Clarence White Telecaster (left) was out in 1993. Missing tuners? Actually, it's two rear-mounted Scruggs detuners. And a tug on the strap would activate a B-string pull device for country bends.

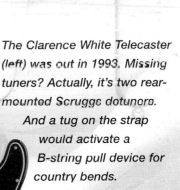

Custom Shop

The Stratocaster turned a mature, sprightly 40 this year, and to mark the occasion Fender issued a stylish 40th Anniversary model, suitably produced in a special limited-edition run of exactly 1,954 instruments. The vintage reissue business was still as busy as ever, underlined in an ad where musicians were invited to travel through time (right). In the meantime, the Strat was still haunted by Jimi's ghost (ad, left).

The Custom Shop was finding more and more of its guitar business was drawn from the regularly produced catalog items it offered. However, starting in 1994 there was a renewed emphasis on one-off productions, and a fresh indulgence of the whims of the select band of Master Builders – the ten or so top luthiers working at the Shop.

The Custom Shop's art guitars are highly decorated instruments – though "objects" might be a better description as it's doubtful that many end up gigged in a sweaty club. More likely they're put on display, much like a piece of sculpture. One of the reasons the Master Builders were encouraged to develop these ultra-fancy pieces was for traveling Fender "art" shows touring the US and Europe, promoting the Custom Shop's capabilities when time and money are not limitations. In this first year, the art guitars included Master Builder Fred Stuart's Egyptian Telecaster, with pyramids and snakes and runes hand-carved by George Amicay in a finish of Corian synthetic stone. There was also the Aloha Strat, for which Master Builder J.T. English had been inspired by Hawaiian art, 1930s resonator guitars, and Art Deco. Ron Chacy engraved the aluminum body, which was colored by Peter Kellit using selective anodizing. A "plain"

aluminum Aloha would become a limited-edition 1995 model dedicated to the memory of the great Fender designer and engineer Freddie Tavares. The necessarily extended period of production of the art guitars made them very expensive. The Shop apparently turned down $75,000 for an "Aztec-Mayan" Tele, while a "Regina del Mare" Strat built in 1997 for Fender's first Catalina Island Blues Festival was sold at a music charity auction for $50,000.

Unusually, the Corona factory rather than the Custom Shop produced a numbered limited edition this year, the 40th Anniversary 1954 Stratocaster (though there was a 40-only run of a Custom Shop Concert Edition). Exactly 1,954 of the factory 40th Strat were made. And American Standard Strats gained a small 40th Anniversary headstock medallion to mark this special year.

Signature models launched included the Dick Dale Strat, recreating the surf king's guitar which he affectionately referred to as The Beast. Jazz-blues stylist Robben Ford had reinterpreted the shortlived 1980s Esprit Ultra as the basis for his signature models, started back in 1989 with some Japan-made instruments. However, from this year the Custom Shop took over production (Ford Ultra model, left).

This Custom Shop "art guitar" was the third Regina Del Mare Strat, made in 1998, for Fender's regular Catalina Island Blues Festival.

Blur's fine Parklife album (below, left) appeared this year, with Graham Coxon (right) often opting for a Tele.

More fanciful Custom Shop fare (below), from a Buffalo Tele to a Flintstones Strat.

Dreams-Come-True

1995
Bash 'em up a bit

Joining the elite club of signature-model endorsers were Bonnie Raitt, Roscoe Beck, Buddy Guy (with polka-dot Strat, above), and Waylon Jennings. More Foto Flame models appeared, looking as if they were made from expensive figured wood thanks to a clever photo-printing technique. And the Relic series was announced, bringing the appeal of aged vintage guitars to new instruments.

Some artists had been asking the Custom Shop to make them a replica of a favorite old guitar or two, usually because the original was much too valuable and cherished to risk taking on the road. But then Keith Richards told the Shop that some replicas made for him for a Stones tour looked too new. "Bash 'em up a bit and I'll play 'em," suggested Richards.

So the Shop began to include wear-and-tear distress marks to replicate the overall look of a battered old original (guitar, that is, not Mr. Richards). Then J.W. Black, a Master Builder at the Custom Shop, came up with the idea of offering these aged replica guitars as regular catalog items, and naming them Relics.

The Shop made two aged 1950s-era samples: a Nocaster (the in-between Broadcaster/Telecaster with no model name) and a "Mary Kaye" Strat (blond body, gold-plated hardware), and announced the new Relic scheme in 1995. Soon the Custom Shop was reacting to the demand generated from these samples by offering a line of three Relic Strats and a Relic Nocaster. The Relics would prove a remarkable success, with the Mary Kaye version becoming the Shop's single best-selling model of the late 1990s.

The line would be expanded from 1998 by offering three types of "re-creations" in what was would be known as the Time Machine series. First are the N.O.S. (New Old Stock) guitars, intended as pristine replicas that are produced as closely as possible to original brand-new instruments that would have come off the

Fender production line during the period at large. Next are the Closet Classics, which are meant to be like guitars bought new years ago, played a little bit… and then shoved under the bed or in a closet. Third is the Relic style, as already mentioned, with "aged" dings and wear added by the Shop.

By 2000 the Custom Shop's Time Machine series would include a '64 Jazz Bass, '51 Nocaster, '59 Precision Bass, '56, '60, and '69 Stratocasters, and a '63 Telecaster – each available in the three different levels of aging, and all listing in the US at around the $2,500 to $3,000 mark. These guitars obviously appeal to a relatively small but growing number of affluent Fender fans, keen to acquire a new Fender with the feel and sound of an oldie and – in the case of the Relics – made to look as if decades of wear-and-tear have stained the fingerboard, scuffed the body, and tarnished the hardware. The Time Machine series is a brilliant move, the nearest Fender has come with new instruments to the almost indefinable appeal of vintage guitars which many thought was firmly and safely locked away in the past.

Also this year, Fender bought the hollowbody guitar maker Guild, gradually rationalizing the lines with an accent on traditional design.

Japanese-made Fender Jaguars and Jazzmasters (above) have been around since 1986, though from 1999 they were only sold in Japan.

This Relic 60s Stratocaster (main guitar) in Daphne Blue was made in 1998.

The first woman with a signature Fender was and still is Bonnie Raitt (above). This one (right) was made in 1999.

Fender recreated its classic ads (left) with the famous "You won't part with yours" tag.

This left-handed Jag-Stang in Fiesta Red was made in 1997.

MEANWHILE IN 1996...

PRIVATIZED TRAINS run in UK for the first time in 50 years.

TWA AIRLINER explodes off Long Island, NY, killing 228.

GLOBE THEATRE "re-opens" in London to present the first Shakespeare performances on the site since 1642.

GIRL POWER declared with Spice Girls debut 'Wannabe.'

ISLAMIC fundamentalists shoot 18 tourists dead in Cairo.

Gunman shoots 35 tourists dead in Port Arthur, Australia.

YASSER ARAFAT elected President of Palestine.

BRITISH BEEF imports cut in 19 countries amid crisis over link between BSE ("mad cow disease") and human CJD.

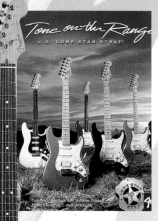

The Lone Star Stratocaster (left) effectively offered an American Standard with hot pickups, including a Seymour Duncan bridge humbucker.

Left-hander Kurt Cobain with his favored live guitar (right), a Mustang with added humbucker. He merged this with a Jaguar to come up with his unusual Jag-Stang.

1996
Jag-shaped Stang

NEW FOR 96

Limited Edition
Richie Sambora "Black Paisley" Stratocaster

The Fender company was 50 years old this year, and a number of celebratory models and promotions marked the occasion (see the ad and anniversary decal, right). Player models included a posthumous hybrid guitar for Kurt Cobain, various Ventures guitars and basses, and Richie Sambora's Japanese black-paisley Strat (left). The hot-pickup Tex Mex Strat, suitably produced at the Mexican factory, was endorsed by Jimmie Vaughan – and became Vaughan's signature model in '97.

Fenders beyond the ubiquitous Strats and Teles were proving popular with so-called grunge guitarists: Seattle supremo Kurt Cobain of Nirvana had played Jaguars and Mustangs; Steve Turner in Mudhoney opted for a Mustang; J. Mascis of Dinosaur Jr. was often seen with his Jazzmaster. And the reason was relatively straightforward. These guitars had the comforting Fender logo on the head, but could be bought more cheaply secondhand than Strats or Teles. The ethics suited grunge perfectly.

Back in 1993, Cobain decided to take cut-up photos of his Jag and Mustang and stick them together, this way and that, trying combinations to see what they would look like. Larry Brooks of the Custom Shop took Cobain's paste-ups, assembled the design, and added a contour or two to improve balance and feel.

After Cobain's untimely death in 1994, his family collaborated with Fender to release a Japanese-made production version of the instrument, named the Fender Jag-Stang. Cobain's guitar hit the market in 1996.

The Lone Star Stratocaster, also launched in 1996, was one example of how the Fender R&D department worked. What it called the core products were taken and subtly (and not-so-subtly) modified to create "new" models based on players' changing tastes. Thus the Lone Star (renamed the American Fat Strat Texas Special in 2000) took an

American Standard Strat and changed the pickup configuration to a Seymour Duncan Pearly Gates Plus humbucker at the bridge, plus two of Fender's "hot" Texas Special single-coils.

Fender marked its 50th anniversary this year. In 1946 Leo Fender had parted company with his original partner, Doc Kauffman. Leo dissolved their K&F company and called his new operation Fender

Manufacturing (and then renamed it the Fender Electric Instrument Co in December 1947). Fender celebrated "50 Years of Excellence" in 1996 with some factory-made limited-edition anniversary models – the apparently timeless quartet of Telecaster, Precision Bass, Stratocaster, and Jazz Bass – with a special commemorative neckplate. Fender also attached a 50th Anniversary decal (see top of page) to many of the general products sold this year.

The Custom Shop made some anniversary models, too, including 50 of the Pine Telecaster & Amp set (above). The guitar recreated the original solidbody prototype with its steel-like headstock shape and angled control plate, while the amp was a replica of an early Model 26, with wooden-handled cabinet and chrome strips over a red felt grille.

If left was right...

Courtney Love saw her Custom Shop Venus model (left) become a Squier production item (far left). Fender went Hendrix crazy with back-to-front and hand-painted Jimi Stratocasters. Also on the loose was a fresh outbreak of Fender merchandizing (catalog, right) bringing logo'd hats, shirts, and jackets – but curiously no Courtney-style outfits.

Almost exactly 30 years since Jimi Hendrix's career had got underway with his debut album, Fender launched a couple of Hendrix-related US-made Strats, from the Custom Shop and the factory.

Corona's contribution was the simply named Jimi Hendrix Stratocaster. The thinking behind the model was anything but simple. Fender had the go-ahead to make an official model in tribute to Hendrix, the best-known Strat player ever. But Jimi was a left-hander and, despite at least ten per cent of us sharing his cackhandedness, the majority of potential customers for such a guitar would want a right-handed machine. Hendrix would take a normal right-handed Strat, turn

it upside down, and re-string it – all to accommodate his left-handedness. So Fender decided to make a completely reversed version of one of Jimi's typical late-1960s Strats. The result is pictured opposite. Right-handed players should consider this as a "normal" left-handed guitar that has been turned upside down and re-strung, thus recreating Jimi's experience in reverse, as it were. As if this was not befuddling enough, Fender added a final flourish, no doubt listening to one of Jimi's great backwards-guitar solos as they did. So that the adoring owner could pose to full effect with the new acquisition in front of the mirror, the normal headstock logo was

applied completely in reverse. In the mirror, you are Jimi. Now all you have to do is master 'Little Wing.'

The Custom Shop's Jimi Hendrix Monterey Strat was more specific. It recreated the hand-painted Strat that Jimi played at the June 1967 Monterey Pop festival… the one that he famously burned on-stage. Careful examination of pictures taken at the show, pre-conflagration, enabled artist Pamelina Hovnatanian to reconstruct Hendrix's flowery painting for the limited edition of 210 guitars.

Fender's other new signature models included one more Hendrix hint: a Jazz Bass for bassman Noel Redding. Hank Marvin and Jimmie Vaughan had Mexican-made Strats, country legend Merle Haggard a Custom Shop Tuff Dog Tele. Guitar combo The Hellecasters had three signatures: Will Ray's Jazz-a-caster, John Jorgensen's Hellecaster, and Jerry Donahue's restrained Strat.

Pickup fiddling continued: the Big Apple was a two-humbucker Strat with single-coil scratch to humbucker raunch (it was renamed the American Double Fat Strat in 2000); the Roadhouse Strat featured three hot Texas Special single-coils (and was renamed the American Strat Texas Special in 2000); and the California series added Tex Mex pickups to US Strats, Teles and P-Basses.

From behind a pile of sartorial memorabilia (right), Jimi smiles at the plight of the right-handed guitarist.

MEANWHILE IN 1997...

O.J. SIMPSON found guilty in civil court case and ordered to pay $15million in punitive damages.

REBELS seize control of Southern Albania, with fighting soon spreading to the capital, Tirana.

WORLD'S OLDEST PERSON Jeanne Caldwell dies at age 122. Also dead this year: Robert Mitchum, James Stewart, William Burroughs, Michael Hutchence, and John Denver.

FUTURISTIC branch of New York's Guggenheim Museum is opened in Bilbao, Spain.

HONG KONG, former British colony, reverts to Chinese rule.

This Jimi Hendrix Stratocaster in Olympic White was produced in 1997.

This Custom Shop Jimi Hendrix Monterey Strat (right) is number 177 of the 210 made during 1997.

Alongside the Venus were two more new Squier guitars, the Super-Sonic (right), and the Jagmaster which was prompted by Bush vocalist Gavin Rossdale's humbucker'd Jazzmaster.

A Japanese-made Ritchie Blackmore signature Strat (ad, above) was out this year.

At the end of the 1990s many guitar-makers were busily looking back to the past for fresh inspiration as the craze for retro flavors seemed to be everywhere. Even the recent Hot Rod Deville and Deluxe amplifiers were now immaculately attired in new tweed cloth (ad, above). Buck Owens twanged a colorful sparkle signature Telecaster (right), and three autographed four-strings appeared: the shortlived Duck Dunn and Geddy Lee P-Basses, plus the Marcus Miller Jazz Bass. All this, and a new US factory too.

Some models were re-organized into new series, with high-end US models grouped as American Deluxes, and reissues together as American Vintages. Retro fever led to the new Toronado and Cyclone (left); upscale, the carved-top Showmasters were Fender's super-est superstrats yet. Fender had recently acquired the De Armond company, famous for old pickups and effects, and began to apply the brand to less expensive Guild-like models from Korea and Indonesia. Fender had owned Guild since 1995.

Biggest event of the year, though, was the opening of a new factory in November, still in Corona, California. The company proudly described the impressive, state-of-the-art plant as the world's most expensive and automated.

Since starting production at the original Corona factory back in 1985, Fender had grown to occupy a total of 115,000 square feet of space in ten buildings across the city. Such a rambling spread proved increasingly inefficient, and Fender began to plan a new centralized factory during the early 1990s. The new $20million 177,000-square-feet plant affords a potentially growing production capacity for the future, and the factory, with a staff of 600, also sees Fender's long-standing tussle with California's stringent environmental laws at an end, as

the new purpose-built paint section is specifically designed to operate without toxic emissions.

Some non-American readers may be confused by references to Fender's "Baja California" factory. This is not the US factory but the Mexican plant which, as we've seen, was established at the end of the 1980s at Ensenada – in an area of Mexico just across the US border known as Baja California.

As the Fender US company neared the 21st century it was using two main sources for Fender-brand instruments: the new Corona factory, and the Mexican plant. Fender Japan's role was dramatically changed, with its continuing high-quality and substantial line almost entirely reserved for sale within Japan, and only a tiny handful of models exported. Fender's move back to an American manufacturer was – for Fender-brand guitars – virtually complete. Fender's new Corona, California, factory may be some 20 miles from Fullerton and the site of Leo Fender's original workshops, but it's a universe away from the humble steel shacks that were Fender's first home. Leo loved few things more than gadgets, and would have been enthralled by the new plant – not least its automated conveyors that supply a vast inventory of guitar components.

This Toronado in Candy Apple Red was made in 1998.

Fender Japan began to sell almost exclusively to its home market, continuing with a large and impressive line that included models such as this Bigsby-equipped Tele (above).

Ex-Miles Davis bassman Marcus Miller had a new signature model based on his own Jazz (pictured).

Past masters

At the close of the 1990s, Fender US used its new California factory and existing Mexican plant as the major sources for Fender-brand instruments, with US-made Jazzmasters and Jaguars (left) appearing for the first time in 20 years or so. Fender Japan too continued to make these and many other models, but now most of its products were sold only in Japan – including these smaller-scale guitars in the 1999 Fender Japan catalog (right).

This was a year of consolidation for Fender after the opening of its new much-expanded factory in Corona at the end of last year. The company also allowed itself – along with most of the rest of the world – to reflect on some past achievements.

A series of ads had started with the tag-line "The Sound That Creates Legends," stressing once again the fact that an impressive line-up of illustrious names had used and were using Fender instruments. (Some examples from the series are illustrated here, including Stevie Ray Vaughan, left.) The Custom Shop reorganized its successful Relics line, the new guitars and basses with which Fender had managed to get closer to the magical appeal of vintage instruments than ever before. Now there were three strands to the series: the original Relic style, given "aged" knocks and wear as if they had been out on the road for a generation or so; the Closet Classic, made to look as if it had been bought new way back when, played a few times, and then stuck in a closet; and N.O.S. (meaning "New Old Stock") which was intended to seem as if an instrument had been bought brand new in the 1950s or 1960s and then put straight into a time machine which transported it to the present day. The kind of thing, in fact, that vintage guitar collectors and dealers regularly fantasize about, but which in real life very rarely happens. Especially the time machine part.

Not only this, but the company had discovered another way of mixing the past with the future. The Fender Museum of Music and The Arts Foundation saw its first full year of operation in 1999, although the doors had actually opened the previous summer. The museum's Executive Director was John Page, who had moved across to the new project from his job as head of the Custom Shop.

At the time of writing the public evidence of the new scheme is a small preview museum, based in Corona, but this is expected to expand rapidly over the coming years. The general aim is to create an impressive museum of the performing arts, and in particular to highlight what Page describes as "Fender's monumental contribution to the world of modern music." This will take the form of exhibits, an archival center, and a Hall of Fame.

The other major strand of the project is educational, and here Fender intends to offer free and low-cost performing-arts teaching. At present this Kids Rock Free program provides lessons for 400 children per week for various instruments and for singing – with a year-and-a-half waiting list – but again this is expected to expand.

This Jaco Pastorius Precision Bass was made in 1999. An aged version, replicating Jaco's own road-weary Jazz, was available from the Custom Shop.

T H E

S O U N D S

T

Our fine four Fender friends – Stratmen Vaughan (opposite), Clapton, Beck, and Hendrix (above) – plus, there in the background, Jazzman Jaco.

C R E A T E

L E G E N D S

Fifty years on from the first Fender solidbodies, those early designs continue to inspire new bands – like Filter (above) with their powerful Tele-and-Strat frontline. Fender tries today to provide models that will appeal to every conceivable type of guitarist and bassist at every level of skill and affluence. Despite the constant references to past achievements (ad, right), the future might well have a new, unimagined direction in store for Fender and for music.

Today, the Fender Musical Instruments Corporation dominates the world's electric guitar market. As we've seen, it's arrived here through a sequence of invention, luck and mishap. Back in the 1950s when the whole adventure started, a Strat was a Strat, and that's what you bought. Now, popular music has fractured into dozens of different factions, each apparently requiring a specific instrument. At the start of 2000 there were 31 distinct factory-made Stratocaster models available. But fifty years is a long time for a company to survive in any business. And Fender has seen its share of shaky times – not least in the earliest days when calamities were regularly avoided by the timely arrival of Leo's wife's salary from the phone company. No doubt Leo would be in awe if he could see the modern Fender operation (though he'd still feel that this or that pickup could be improved). It was his sheer determination – today it would be described as workaholism – that determined much of the company's early direction. Of course, he listened to what musicians had to say to him. And he assembled a first-rate team: the Don Randalls and Freddie Tavares's and Forrest Whites of those crucial, ground-breaking days in Fullerton. No other guitar-making company has

scored with such an impressive trio of early products. The Telecaster, as it quickly became known, is a historic instrument: the world's first modern commercially-available solidbody electric Spanish guitar. The Stratocaster is the most influential solidbody design ever, beating even Gibson's mighty Les Paul into second place. And Fender's most revolutionary product was the Precision Bass, the first commercial electric bass guitar and an instrument that changed the sound of popular music.

And all that within four years. More models followed on in the wake of that great trio, of course: a few were very good, some were clearly bad, others simply indifferent. But Fender's sheer exhilarating invention between 1950 and 1954 is astounding. All musicians, all guitar-makers, all music fans are in debt to what Leo Fender and his team achieved in those years.

Back in 1950 – a year of innocence and excitement at Fender as that first solidbody guitar began to appear – someone from the small band of people working at the company wrote a short note in the catalog. "The Fender people hope to always be close to the feelings of those who buy, sell and play electric instruments," it said, "because that is the greatest source of information for the development and improvement of instruments." Nothing much has changed since, and yet everything has changed.

A limited-run "aged" Custom Shop guitar (right) was made this year in tribute to Muddy Waters and his Telecaster.

MEANWHILE AT THE MILLENNIUM

IN LONDON thousands watch as the "river of fire" fails to light.

IN JAPAN millions head for Buddhist temples and Shinto shrines to wish for good fortune in the Year of the Dragon.

IN GIZA an "electronic opera" by Jean-Michel Jarre begins Egypt's missable millennium show.

EXPLORER Michel Siffre, underground for over a month with no means of telling time, thinks it is still December 27th.

PROPHECIES For A New Millennium has James Manning predicting a future of inclement weather and mass deaths.

MORE OF THE SAME on December 31st 2999.

This Leo Fender Broadcaster, #44 of 50, marked the model's 50th anniversary. A certificate and documents (above right) came with it.

The D'Aquisto Classic Rocker (opposite) was a Gretsch-like hollowbody, new for 2000.

The mix of old and new continues: Thom Yorke of Radiohead is pictured (above) with a 70s-style Tele Deluxe.

chronology 1950-2000

This listing is designed to show in chronological order the production-model electric guitars and basses that have "Fender" as their main logo/brandname, and that have been manufactured in the US, Japan, Korea, and Mexico between 1950 and summer 2000.

The start date shown is the year that production commenced for each model in the country of manufacture, regardless of eventual availability elsewhere (if any such difference is applicable). The finish date is the final year that each model was available in the US and/or Europe. Some Japanese-made examples did and do continue in production beyond the stated dates, but these are intended for sale in Japan only.

Model	Dates
Broadcaster	50-51
Esquire (1-p/up production model)	51-69
"Nocaster"	51
Precision Bass (1st ver.)	51-57
Telecaster	51-82
Stratocaster (1st ver.)	54-64
Duo-Sonic (1st ver., short scale)	56-64
Musicmaster (1st ver., short scale)	56-64
Precision Bass (2nd ver., split p/up)	57-81
Jazzmaster	58-80
Custom Esquire (bound body)	59-69
Custom Telecaster (bound body)	59-72
Jazz Bass (1st ver., stacked controls)	60-62
VI (aka "Bass VI") (1st ver., 3 switches)	61-63
Jaguar	62-75
Jazz Bass (2nd ver., 3 controls)	62-75
VI (aka "Bass VI") (2nd ver., 4 switches)	63-75
Duo-Sonic (2nd ver., short scale)	64-69
Duo-Sonic II (normal scale)	64-69
Musicmaster (2nd ver., short scale)	64-69
Musicmaster II (normal scale)	64-69
Mustang (normal scale)	64-81

Model	Dates
Mustang (short scale)	64-69
Bass V	65-70
Electric XII	65-69
Stratocaster (2nd ver., enlarged h/stock)	65-71
Coronado I	66-69
Coronado I Bass	66-68
Coronado II	66-69
Coronado XII	66-69
Mustang Bass	66-81
Slab-Body Precision Bass	66-67
Antigua Coronado II	67-71
Antigua Coronado XII	67-71
Bronco	67-80
Coronado II Bass	67-69
Wildwood Coronado II	67-69
Wildwood Coronado II Bass	67-69
Wildwood Coronado XII	67-69
Antigua Coronado II Bass	68-71
Blue Flower Telecaster	68-69
Blue Flower Telecaster Bass	68-69
"Competition" Mustang	68-73
"Competition" Mustang Bass	68-73
LTD	68-74
Montego I	68-74
Montego II	68-74
Paisley Red Telecaster	68-69
Paisley Red Telecaster Bass	68-69
Telecaster Bass (1st ver., single-coil p/up)	68-72
Thinline Telecaster (1st ver.)	68-71

Model	Dates
Custom (aka Maverick)	69-70
Musicmaster (2nd ver., normal scale)	69-75
Rosewood Telecaster	69-72
Swinger (aka "Arrow" or "Musiclander")	69
Musicmaster Bass	70-81
Stratocaster (3rd ver., 3-bolt neck)	71-81
Thinline Telecaster (2nd ver.)	71-79
Telecaster Bass (2nd ver., h/bucker p/up)	72-79
Telecaster Custom (with h/bucker)	72-81
Telecaster Deluxe	73-81
Jazz Bass (3rd ver., 3-bolt neck)	75-81
Musicmaster (3rd ver.)	75-80
"Rhinestone" Stratocaster (UK only)	75
Starcaster	76-80
"Antigua" Jazz Bass	77-79
"Antigua" Mustang	77-79
"Antigua" Mustang Bass	77-79
"Antigua" Precision Bass	77-79
"Antigua" Stratocaster	77-79
"Antigua" Telecaster	77-79
"Antigua" Telecaster Custom	77-79
"Antigua" Telecaster Deluxe	77-79
Lead I	79-82
Lead II	79-82
25th Anniversary Stratocaster	79-80